love to knit

Bronwyn Lowenthal

love to knit

25 quick and stylish fashion projects you will love to knit

CICO BOOKS

LONDON NEW YORK

Published in 2007 by CICO Books
an imprint of Ryland Peters & Small
519 Broadway, 5th Floor, New York, NY 10012

10 9 8 7 6 5 4 3 2 1

Text and project designs © Bronwyn Lowenthal 2007
Design and photography © CICO Books 2007

A CIP catalog record for this book is available from the
Library of Congress

ISBN-13: 978 1 906094 03 4
ISBN-10: 1 906094 03 9

Printed in China

Editor: Kate Haxell
Designer: Luis Peral-Aranda
Photographer: Becky Maynes
Additional photography credits on page 128

contents

introduction

My love affair with handicrafts started after meeting an eccentric traveller on my very first day of a round–the–world trip beginning in Bali. Although the Balinese are not big knitters (being more into weaving and carving), my consciousness of human creativity was aroused and I started to notice handiwork wherever I went. It was on a trip to Turkey, where little hands can often knit before they can write, that I became fascinated by woolcrafts and specifically knitting.

This first trip to Turkey inspired me to give up my day job and start my own knitwear-based fashion label called *Lowie*. As I got stuck into being a fashion designer, I noticed that so many of the knitting books available were a bit, well, "grandma." I've nothing against grandmas (I've had two of my own), but surely, now that knitting was cool again, younger knitters would want to make some more fashionable items, or at least something that was less "grandma" and more "granny chic."

Some of the items in this book are favorites from past Lowie collections and other pieces have been designed specifically and exclusively for this, my first knitting book. There are super-simple projects, like the Armwarmers on page 16 that are perfect for beginners, while seasoned knitters will relish the more intricate projects, such as the Trapeze Jacket on page 80. My designs, I hope, have a sense of humor and fun about them that means you'll love to knit them. In this book you'll find lots of quirky young pieces to wear, which I've certainly had fun designing.

I encourage you to explore your own boundaries of creativity, particularly when it come to embellishments, so we've added a special embellishments section on pages 88–97. And if you are a novice knitter, you'll find all the techniques you need on pages 98–121.

Explore your love to knit.

Bronwyn Lowenthal

hands up

short and long fleur-de-lys gloves

Who could resist these lovely vintage-look fingerless gloves? There are short and long versions, so knit the ones you prefer. Stretchy velvet ribbon makes it easy to get your hand into the glove, but if you can't find it, tie the bow so it fits the widest part of your hand.

SIZE

8¾in around hand

YARN SUGGESTION

1 1¾oz ball of bulky-weight yarn (such as Rowan Little Big Wool) in main color (M)

1 1¾oz ball of bulky-weight yarn (such as Rowan Little Big Wool) in contrast color (C)

NEEDLES

Pair of US 9 knitting needles
Knitter's sewing needle

OTHER MATERIALS

52in of 1-in wide stretchy velvet ribbon

GAUGE

16 stitches and 22 rows to 4in square over stockinette stitch using US 9 needles.

ABBREVIATIONS

See page 120.

PATTERN (short gloves)

LEFT GLOVE

**Using M, cast on 33 sts.

Row 1 (RS): *K1, p1, rep from * to last st, k1.

Rep row 1 fifteen more times.

Row 17 (eyelet row): K1, *yo, k2tog, rep from * to end.

Change to C.

Row 18: Purl.

Row 19: Knit

Row 20: Purl.

Rep rows 19–20 three more times.**

Divide for thumb

Row 27: K16, turn, p6, turn, cast on 6 sts.

***Starting with a knit row, work 4 rows st st on these 12 sts.

Bind off.

Join thumb seam.

With right-side facing and starting at division of thumb, rejoin yarn, pick up and knit 6 sts from cast on sts at base of thumb, k to end.

Starting with a purl row, work 4 rows st st across all sts.

Bind off.***

RIGHT GLOVE

Work from ** to ** of Left Glove.

Divide for thumb

Row 27: K23, turn, p6, turn, cast on 6 sts.

Work from *** to *** of Left Glove to complete.

FINISHING

Join side seam neatly.

Following chart on page 13 and main photograph and working with cuff facing away from you, Swiss-darn fleur-de-lys patterns onto C part of gloves, using M.

Cut ribbon into two equal lengths. Thread one length of ribbon through eyelets in each glove and tie in bow on front.

" muted colors
give these gloves
a vintage look "

PATTERN (long gloves)

LEFT GLOVE

**Using M, cast on 33 sts.

Row 1 (RS): *K1, p1, rep from * to last st, k1.

Rep row 1 fifteen more times.

Row 17 (eyelet row): K1, *yo, k2tog, rep from * to end.

Row 18: *K1, p1, rep to last st, k1.

Row 19: *P1, k1, rep to last st, p1.

Row 20: Purl.

Row 21: Knit

Row 22: Purl.

Rep rows 21–22 three more times.**

Divide for thumb

Row 29: K16, turn, p6, turn, cast on 6 sts.

***Starting with a knit row, work 6 rows st st on these 12 sts.

Bind off.

Join thumb seam.

With right-side facing and starting at division of thumb, rejoin yarn, pick up and knit 6 sts from cast on sts at base of thumb, k to end.

Starting with a purl row, work 10 rows st st across all sts.

Bind off.***

RIGHT GLOVE

Work from ** to ** of Left Glove.

Divide for thumb

Row 29: K23, turn, p6, turn, cast on 6 sts.

Work from *** to *** of Left Glove to complete.

FINISHING

Join side seam neatly.

Following chart below and main photograph and working with cuff facing away from you, Swiss-darn fleur-de-lys patterns onto C part of gloves, using M.

Cut ribbon into two equal lengths. Thread one length of ribbon through eyelets in each glove and tie in bow on front.

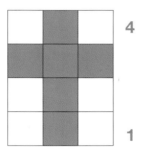

4

1

Chart for Swiss-darned fleur-de-lys motif.

SIZE

8¾in around hand

YARN SUGGESTION

2 1¾oz balls of bulky-weight yarn (such as Rowan Little Big Wool) in main color (M)

Small amount of bulky-weight yarn (such as Rowan Little Big Wool) in contrast color (C) for embroidery

NEEDLES

Pair of US 9 knitting needles
Knitter's sewing needle

OTHER MATERIALS

52in of 1-in wide stretchy velvet ribbon

GAUGE

16 stitches and 22 rows to 4in square over stockinette stitch using US 9 needles.

ABBREVIATIONS

See page 120.

cabled mittens

Thread the mitten cord through your coat sleeves, then when you go into your favorite boutique, slip off the mittens and leave them dangling, without the risk of losing them while you make important purchases.

SIZE

7½in around hand

YARN SUGGESTION

2 1¾oz balls of bulky-weight yarn (such as Rowan Cashsoft Chunky)
1 1¾oz ball of fingering-weight yarn (such as Rowan Cashsoft 4-ply)

NEEDLES

Set of 4 double-pointed US 9 knitting needles
2 double-pointed US 2 knitting needles or French knitting bobbin
Cable needle
Stitch holders
Knitter's sewing needle

GAUGE

16 stitches and 22 rows to 4in square over stockinette stitch using bulky-weight yarn and US 9 needles.

ABBREVIATIONS

C6B = slip next 3 sts onto cable needle and leave at back of work, k3, then k3 from cable needle.
C6F = slip next 3 sts onto cable needle and leave at front of work, k3, then k3 from cable needle.
See also page 120.

PATTERN

RIGHT MITTEN

Using bulky-weight yarn and US 9 needles, cast on 28 sts and distribute them evenly over 3 needles (10 sts on 2 needles, and 8 sts on 3rd needle.) Using 4th needle, work in rounds as folls:

Round 1: *K2, p2, rep from * to end. Rep this round seven more times.

Round 9: K5, inc in next st, k14, inc in next st, k3, inc in next st, k3. *31 sts*
Now work in cable patt as folls:

Rounds 10–12: Knit.

Round 13: K3, C6B, k to end.

Rounds 14–16: Knit.

Round 17: K6, C6F, k to end.
Rounds 10–17 form cable patt.
Work in patt for 15 more rounds.

Shape thumb

Slip first 15 sts and last 10 sts of last round onto a holder but do NOT break yarn.

**With RS facing, join in new ball of yarn to rem 6 sts and cont as folls:

Next round: Cast on and knit 6 sts, k6. *12 sts*
Distribute these 12 sts evenly over 3 needles (4 sts on each needle) and, using 4th needle, work in rounds as folls:

Next round: Knit.
Rep this round ten more times.

Next round: [Skpo, k2, k2tog] twice. *8 sts*

Next round: [Skpo, k2tog] twice. *4 sts*
Break yarn and thread through rem 4 sts. Pull up tight and fasten off.

Return to sts left on stitch holder before shaping thumb and, using yarn left with last round worked, cont as folls:

Round 33: Patt 15 sts, pick up and knit 6 sts from base of thumb, patt to end. Distribute these 31 sts evenly over 3 needles and, using 4th needle, cont in cable patt as set as folls:
Work 17 rounds.**

Shape top

Round 51: K1, skpo, patt 9 sts, k2tog, k2, skpo, k10, k2tog, k1. *27 sts*

Round 52: K1, skpo, k7, k2tog, k2, skpo, k8, k2tog, k1. *23 sts*

Round 53: K1, skpo, k5, k2tog, k2, skpo, k6, k2tog, k1. *19 sts*

Round 54: K1, skpo, k3, k2tog, k2, skpo, k4, k2tog, k1. *15 sts*

Round 55: K1, skpo, k1, k2tog, k2, skpo, k2, k2tog, k1. *11 sts*

Round 56: K1, skpo, k3, skpo, k2tog, k1. *8 sts*

Break yarn and thread through rem 8 sts. Pull up tight and fasten off.

LEFT MITTEN

Using bulky-weight yarn and US 9 needles, cast on 28 sts and distribute them evenly over 3 needles (10 sts on 2 needles, and 8 sts on 3rd needle.) Using 4th needle, work in rounds as folls:

Round 1: *P2, k2, rep from * to end. Rep this round seven more times.

Round 9: K6, inc in next st, k3, inc in next st, k7, inc in next st, k9. *31 sts*
Now work in cable patt as folls:

Rounds 10–12: Knit.
Round 13: K19, C6B, k to end.
Rounds 14–16: Knit.
Round 17: K22, C6F, k to end.
Rounds 10–17 form cable patt.
Work in patt for 15 more rounds.

Shape thumb
Slip first 10 sts and last 15 sts of last round onto a holder but do NOT break yarn.
Work as Right Mitten from ** to **.

Shape top
Round 51: K1, skpo, k10, k2tog, k2, skpo, patt 9 sts, k2tog, k1. *27 sts*
Round 52: K1, skpo, k8, k2tog, k2, skpo, k7, k2tog, k1. *23 sts*
Round 53: K1, skpo, k6, k2tog, k2, skpo, k5, k2tog, k1. *19 sts*
Round 54: K1, skpo, k4, k2tog, k2, skpo, k3, k2tog, k1. *15 sts*
Round 55: K1, skpo, k2, k2tog, k2, skpo, k1, k2tog, k1. *11 sts*
Round 56: K1, skpo, k2tog, k3, k2tog, k1. *8 sts*
Break yarn and thread through rem 8 sts. Pull up tight and fasten off.

CORD
Cast on 6 sts using fingering-weight yarn and US 2 needles.
Row 1: K6, *without turning work slip these 6 sts to opposite end of needle and bring yarn to opposite end of work pulling it quite tightly across WS of work, knit these 6 sts again, rep from * until string is 63in long.
Bind off.
Alternatively, use the fingering-weight yarn to make a length of French knitting or a twisted cord (see page 96), to join the mittens.

FINISHING
Darn in ends neatly, then press carefully. Attach ends of string to inside of cast on edge of each mitten at beginning of first round.

armwarmers

These warmers will keep your arms cozy in three-quarter-sleeved coats and tops. I've done a super-simple thumbless pattern and a version with easy-to-work thumbs. The armwarmers are fitted, so they will also work well under long-sleeved coats.

PATTERN

(both alike)
Cast on 30 sts and divide the sts evenly over 3 needles.
Place marker to indicate beg of round.
Round 1: *K1, p1, rep from * to end.
Rep round 1 seven more times.
Round 9: *K4, p1, rep from * to end.
Rep round 9 until work measures 15¼in.
Bind off.

For armwarmers with thumbs, work as given for Armwarmers until work measures 12in, then work as folls, keeping k4, p1, patt correct:

RIGHT ARMWARMER
Next round: Patt 15, slip next 6 sts onto a holder, patt 9 sts.
Next round: Patt 15, cast on 6 sts, patt 9 sts.
Work rounds in patt until work measures 15¼in.
Bind off.
Shape thumb
Rejoin yarn to cast on sts.
Pick up and knit 6 sts across cast on sts, knit 6 sts from holder.
Divide sts evenly over 3 needles.
Work 8 rounds st st.
Bind off.

LEFT ARMWARMER
Next round: Patt 9, slip next 6 sts onto a holder, patt 15 sts.
Next round: Patt 9, cast on 6 sts, patt 15 sts.
Work rounds in patt until work measures 15¼in.
Bind off.
Shape thumb
Rejoin yarn to cast on sts.
Pick up and knit 6 sts across cast on sts, knit 6 sts from holder.
Divide sts evenly over 3 needles.
Work 8 rounds st st.
Bind off.

SIZE

One size

YARN SUGGESTION

2 1¾oz balls of worsted-weight yarn (such as Debbie Bliss Merino Aran)

NEEDLES

Set of 4 double-pointed US 10 knitting needles
Round marker
Stitch holders

GAUGE

18 stitches and 24 rows to 4in square over patt (unstretched) using US 10 needles.

ABBREVIATIONS

See page 120.

lacy long gloves

These are in the same stitch pattern as the shawl on page 46, and the two work well worn together. I find cotton lace trimming has a more upmarket feel and is easy to dye if you want to get creative. Wear the gloves over tight-fitting leather ones on chilly evenings.

SIZE

6¼in around hand

YARN SUGGESTION

2 ¾oz balls of fine kid mohair yarn (such as Rowan Kidsilk Haze)

NEEDLES

Pair of US 6 knitting needles
Set of 4 double-pointed US 6 knitting needles
Stitch holders
Round marker
Knitter's sewing needle

OTHER MATERIALS

39in of ¾-in wide cotton lace
6 buttons

GAUGE

21 stitches and 22 rows to 4in square over patt using 2 strands of yarn held together and US 6 needles.

ABBREVIATIONS

See page 120.

PATTERN

RIGHT GLOVE
Using 2 strands of yarn held together and US 6 needles, cast on 39 sts loosely.
Row 1: P1, *k1, p1, rep from * to end.
Row 2: K1, *p1, k1, rep from * to end.
These 2 rows form rib.
Work in rib for 2 rows more.
Row 5: Rib to last 3 sts, yo, k2tog (for first buttonhole), p1.
Work in rib for a further 2 rows.
Row 8: Rib 4, [work 2 tog, rib 5] five times. *34 sts*
Row 9: [P2, k9, k3tog, yo, k1, yo] twice, p1, yo, k2tog (for 2nd buttonhole), k1.
Row 10: P2, k2, [p13, k2] twice.
Row 11: *P2, k7, k3tog, [k1, yo] twice, k1, rep from * once more, p2, k2.
Row 12: As row 10.
Row 13: [P2, k5, k3tog, k2, yo, k1, yo, k2] twice, p1, yo, k2tog (for 3rd buttonhole), k1.
Row 14: As row 10.
Row 15: [P2, k3, k3tog, k3, yo, k1, yo, k3] twice, p2, k2.
Row 16: As row 10.
This completes cuff opening.
Now distribute the 34 sts evenly over 3 of the double-pointed US 6 needles, place marker and, using 4th needle, work in rounds in lacy patt as folls:
Round 1: [P2, yo, k1, yo, sl 1, k2tog, psso, k9] twice, p2, k2.
Round 2 and every foll alt round: [P2, k13] twice, p2, k2.

Round 3: *P2, [k1, yo] twice, k1, sl 1, k2tog, psso, k7, rep from * once more, p2, k2.
Round 5: [P2, k2, yo, k1, yo, k2, sl 1, k2tog, psso, k5] twice, p2, k2.
Round 7: [P2, k3, yo, k1, yo, k3, sl 1, k2tog, psso, k3] twice, p2, k2.
Round 9: [P2, k9, k3tog, yo, k1, yo] twice, p2, k2.
Round 11: *P2, k7, k3tog, [k1, yo] twice, k1, rep from * once more, p2, k2.
Round 13: [P2, k5, k3tog, k2, yo, k1, yo, k2] twice, p2, k2.
Round 15: [P2, k3, k3tog, k3, yo, k1, yo, k3] twice, p2, k2.
Round 16: As round 2.
These 16 rounds form lacy patt.
Work in lacy patt for a further 52 rounds.

Shape thumb

Slip first 7 sts and last 19 sts of last round onto a holder but do NOT break yarn.
With RS facing, join in new ball of yarn to rem 8 sts and cont as folls:
Next round: Cast on and knit 8 sts, k8. *16 sts*
Distribute these 16 sts evenly over 3 needles (5 sts on 2 needles, and 6 on 3rd needle) and, using 4th needle, work in rounds as folls:
Next round: Knit.
Rep this round eight more times.
Bind off.
Return to sts left on holder before shaping thumb and, using yarn left with last round worked, cont as folls:
Next round: Patt 7 sts, pick up and knit

8 sts from base of thumb, patt to end.
Distribute these 34 sts evenly over 3 needles and, using 4th needle, cont in lacy patt for a further 13 rounds.
Bind off.

LEFT GLOVE
Using 2 strands of yarn held together and US 6 needles, cast on 39 sts loosely.
Work in rib as given for Right Glove for 4 rows.
Row 5: P1, k1, yo, k2tog (for first buttonhole), rib to end.
Work in rib for a further 2 rows.
Row 8: Rib 4, [work 2 tog, rib 5] five times. *34 sts*
Row 9: K2, yo (for 2nd buttonhole), p2tog, [k9, k3tog, yo, k1, yo, p2] twice.
Row 10: K2, [p13, k2] twice, p2.
Row 11: K2, *p2, k7, k3tog, [k1, yo] twice, k1, rep from * once more, p2.
Row 12: As row 10.
Row 13: K2, yo, p2tog (for 3rd buttonhole), [k5, k3tog, k2, yo, k1, yo, k2, p2] twice.
Row 14: As row 10.
Row 15: K2, [p2, k3, k3tog, k3, yo, k1, yo, k3] twice, p2.
Row 16: As row 10.
This completes cuff opening.
Now distribute the 34 sts evenly over 3 of the double-pointed US 6 needles, place marker and, using 4th needle, work in rounds in lacy patt as folls:
Round 1: K2, [p2, yo, k1, yo, sl 1, k2tog, psso, k9] twice, p2.
Round 2 and every foll alt round: K2, [p2, k13] twice, p2.
Round 3: K2, *p2, [k1, yo] twice, k1, sl 1, k2tog, psso, k7, rep from * once more, p2.
Round 5: K2, [p2, k2, yo, k1, yo, k2, sl 1, k2tog, psso, k5] twice, p2.
Round 7: K2, [p2, k3, yo, k1, yo, k3, sl 1, k2tog, psso, k3] twice, p2.
Round 9: K2, [p2, k9, k3tog, yo, k1, yo] twice, p2.
Round 11: K2, *p2, k7, k3tog, [k1, yo] twice, k1, rep from * once more, p2.
Round 13: K2, [p2, k5, k3tog, k2, yo, k1, yo, k2] twice, p2.
Round 15: K2, [p2, k3, k3tog, k3, yo, k1, yo, k3] twice, p2.
Round 16: As round 2.
These 16 rounds form lacy patt.
Work in lacy patt for a further 52 rounds.

Shape thumb
Slip first 19 sts and last 7 sts of last round onto a holder but do NOT break yarn.
With RS facing, join in new ball of yarn to rem 8 sts and cont as folls:
Next round: Cast on and knit 8 sts, k8. *16 sts*
Distribute these 16 sts evenly over 3 needles (5 sts on 2 needles, and 6 on 3rd needle) and, using 4th needle, work in rounds as folls:
Next round: Knit.
Rep this round eight more times.
Bind off.
Return to sts left on holder before shaping thumb and, using yarn left with last round worked, cont as folls:
Next round: Patt 19 sts, pick up and knit 8 sts from base of thumb, patt to end.
Distribute these 34 sts evenly over 3 needles and, using 4th needle, cont in lacy patt for a further 13 rounds.
Bind off.

FINISHING
Darn in ends neatly, then press carefully. Attach buttons to correspond with buttonholes. Cut lace into two equal lengths and run gathering threads along straight edge. Using photograph as a guide and pulling up gathering threads to fit, sew lace in place around cuff opening and cast on edge.

"wear these gloves with the lacy shawl on page 46"

feet first

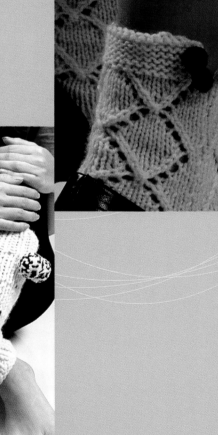

"the most comfortable of chunky winter socks"

turkish socks

It's because of these socks that I fell in love with knitwear and became a knitwear designer. On my first holiday to Turkey I bought several pairs of these socks—all slightly different—and gave them to my friends. One friend in particular loved them so much that she was wearing them almost every time I came to visit. They are certainly the most comfortable of chunky winter socks and are just as fabulous for lounging in front of the TV as they are worn with Birkenstocks, sandals, rubber boots, or clogs.

You can easily make these socks from any little scraps of sport-weight yarn left hanging around. Try raiding a friend's yarn stash or your local thrift store.

PATTERN

(both alike)

Using A, cast on 44 sts. Arrange the sts so that there are 16 sts on one needle and 14 sts on each of 2 needles.

Place a marker to indicate start of rounds.

Being careful not to twist the sts, join into the round.

Round 1: *K3, p1, rep from * to end.

Rep round 1 until work measures 2¾in from cast on, inc 1 st at end of last round. *45 sts*

Knit 2 rounds.

Start Chart A (see page 27.)

Knit 1 round.

Next round: *K3M, k2B, rep from * to end.

Complete Chart A.

Change to C

Knit 1 round, inc 3 sts evenly. *48 sts*

Change to D

**Start Chart B (see page 27.)

Knit 1 round.

Next round: *K3D, k3E, rep from * to end.

Complete Chart B.

Change to C

Start Chart C (see page 27.)

Knit 1 round.

Complete Chart C.**

Rep from ** to **, changing colors for Chart B as indicated by main photograph,

SIZE

Approximately 8¾in from heel to toe (unstretched)

YARN SUGGESTION

1 1¾oz ball of sport-weight yarn (such as Rowan Pure Wool DK) in each of variegated gray (A), purple (B), black (C), red (D), green (E), white (F), turquoise (G), pale green (H) and orange (J)

NEEDLES

Set of 4 double-pointed US 6 knitting needles
Round marker
Knitter's sewing needle

GAUGE

22 stitches and 28 rows to 4in square over stockinette stitch using US 6 needles.

ABBREVIATIONS

See page 120.

Note: work patterns using the Fair Isle technique, stranding yarns not in use loosely across the back.

until work measures 12¾in from cast on, ending with last round of Chart C.

Divide for heel

Change to H

Next row: K11H, slip last 12 sts of round onto other end of same needle (these 23 sts are for the heel.) Divide rem sts onto 2 needles and leave for instep.

Next row: Purl.

Next row: Knit

Next row: Purl

Next row: Knit, bring in J and work as row 3 of Chart A, ending with 1J, 2H.

Next row: Purl, cont Chart A.

Next row: Knit, change background color to E and cont Chart A.

Next row: Purl, cont Chart A.

Break J, work in E only.

Next row: Knit.

Next row: Purl.

Next row: Knit, dec 1 st at each end. *21 sts*

Next row: Purl, dec 1 st at each end. *19 sts*

Rep last two rows until 5 sts remain.

Cont in st st, inc 1 st at each end of every row until there are 23 sts.

Work 2 rows straight.

Next row: Knit, bring in J and work as row 3 of Chart A, ending with 1J, 2H.

Next row: Purl, cont Chart A.

Next row: Knit, change background color to H and cont Chart A.

Next row: Purl, cont Chart A.

Break J, work in H only

Work 3 rows st st.

Work 1 row in C.

Now divide sts so that there are 12 sts on 1st needle, 24 sts on 2nd needle and 12 sts on 3rd needle.

Work in rounds, placing marker as before to indicate start of rounds.

Rep from ** to **, changing colors for Chart B as indicated by main photograph, until work measures 4½in from heel shaping, ending with first row of Chart C.

Shape toe

At the same time as working decs as set, work Chart A in C and G, rep rounds 1–5 only.

Next round: Knit to last 3 sts on 1st needle, k2tog, k1, on 2nd needle k1, k2togtbl, k to last 3 sts, k2tog, k1, on 3rd needle k1, k2togtbl, k to end.

Rep last round nine more times. *8 sts*

Break yarn, thread through rem sts and close, forming a flat toe.

FINISHING

Join heel side seams neatly.

charts

Place these charts as instructed in the pattern.

A

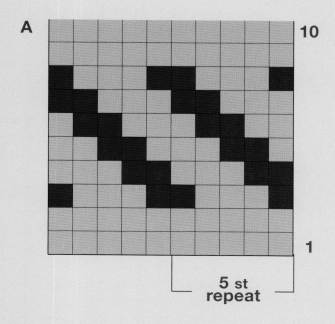

10

1

5 st
repeat

B

10

1

6 st
repeat

C

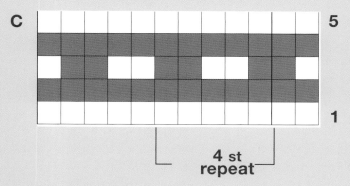

5

1

4 st
repeat

2-button small socks

Cute and sexy! Wooly socks are certainly not just for sleeptime: here, they are dressed up with heels and contrast buttons. However, they will work equally well for summer in cotton or silk-blend yarns and you could certainly wear them with strappy sandals or trainers, and a pair of shorts or a little summer dress.

SIZE

Approximately 8in from heel to toe (unstretched)

YARN SUGGESTION

2 1¾oz balls of sport-weight yarn (such as Rowan Pure Wool DK)

NEEDLES

Pair of US 2 knitting needles
Stitch holders
Knitter's sewing needle

OTHER MATERIALS

4 small buttons
Sewing needle and thread

GAUGE

25 stitches and 35 rows to 4in square over lace patt using US 2 needles.

ABBREVIATIONS

See page 120.

PATTERN

Lace patt
Row 1: K2, *yo, skpo, k5, k2tog, yo, k1, rep from * to last st, k1.
Row 2 and foll 6 alt rows: Purl.
Row 3: K3, *yo, skpo, k3, k2tog, yo, k3, rep from * to end.
Row 5: K4, *yo, skpo, k1, k2tog, yo, k5, rep from *, ending last rep, k4.
Row 7: K5, *yo, sl 1, k2tog, psso, yo, k7, rep from *, ending last rep, k5.
Row 9: K4, *k2tog, yo, k1, yo, skpo, k5, rep from *, ending last rep, k4.
Row 11: K3, *k2tog, yo, k3, yo, skpo, k3, rep from * to end.
Row 13: K2, *k2tog, yo, k5, yo, skpo, k1, rep from * to last st, k1.
Row 15: K1, k2tog, yo, k7,*yo, sl 1, k2tog, psso, yo, k7, rep from * to last 3 sts, yo, skpo, k1.
Row 16: Purl.
These 16 rows form lace patt and are repeated.

RIGHT SOCK
Cast on 49 sts.
Knit 2 rows.
Row 3 (RS): K2, yo, k2tog, k to end.
Knit 3 rows.
Row 7: As row 3.
Knit 3 rows.
Row 11: Bind off 6 sts, then work lace patt starting with row 1 (the stitch on the right-hand needle counts as the first knit stitch.)
Cont until 40 rows of lace patt have been completed.
Next row: Patt 23 sts, turn, place rem 20 sts on stitch holder.
Cont in patt until 75 rows of lace patt in total have been completed.
Knit 1 row.
Shape toe
Work in st st (1 row knit, 1 row purl), starting with a knit row.
Dec 1 st at each end of next and every alt row until 13 sts rem.
Work 1 row.
Bind off.
Shape heel
Rejoin yarn to 20 sts on stitch holder.
With right side facing, knit 1 row, inc 1 st at each end and 1 st in the center.
23 sts
Work 11 rows st st without shaping.
**Next row: K14, k2tog, turn, *sl 1 purlwise, p5, p2tog, turn, sl 1 knitwise, k5, k2tog, turn, rep from * until 7 sts rem.
Next row: K7, pick up and knit 8 sts down heel.
Next row: P15, pick up and purl 8 sts down other side of heel.
Cont in st st until work measures same as top of sock to start of toe shaping.

Shape toe

Work in st st, starting with a knit row.
Dec 1 st at each end of next and
every alt row until 13 sts rem.
Work 1 row.
Bind off.

LEFT SOCK

Cast on 49 sts.
Knit 1 row.
Row 2: K2, yo, k2tog, k to end.
Knit 3 rows.
Rep last 4 rows once more.
Row 10: Bind off 6 sts, k to end.
Work 40 rows of lace patt.
Next row: K20, patt 23 sts.
Next row: P23, turn, place rem 20 sts
on stitch holder.
Cont in patt until 75 rows of lace patt
in total have been completed.
Knit 1 row.

Shape toe

Work in st st, starting with a knit row.
Dec 1 st at each end of next and
every alt row until 13 sts rem.
Work 1 row.
Bind off.

Shape heel

Rejoin yarn to 20 sts on stitch holder.
With wrong side facing, purl 1 row, inc
1 st at each end and 1 st in the
center. *23 sts*
Work 10 rows st st without shaping.
Work as Right Sock from ** to
complete.

FINISHING

Join foot and side seams neatly. Sew
two buttons to garter stitch cuff to
align with eyelet buttonholes.

"wear these
socks with strappy
sandals and shorts
for summer"

"the legwarmers
of your dreams
in any color you
can dream of"

v-spot legwarmers

I love these legwarmers: they are surely some of the cutest ever created. Wear them over jeans, with a thick pair of tights, or with flip flops and pushed down to the ankles on a summer evening. If you want to be really fashionable you could even use them as fat armwarmers or, for an 80s fix, double the length and wear them thigh-high. Don't be afraid to get creative with fun color combinations.

PATTERN

(both alike)
Using M, cast on 32 sts.
Row 1 (RS): *K1, p1, rep from * to end.
Rep row 1 nine more times.
Row 11: Knit.
Row 12: Purl.
Rep rows 11–12 twice more.
Row 17: K3M, *k1C, k3M, rep from * to last st, k1M.
Rows 18–25: Work st st in M.
Row 26: P2M, *p1C, p3M, rep from * to last 2 sts, p1C, p1M.
Rows 27–34: Work st st in M.
Rep rows 17–34 once more.
Rep rows 17–25 once more.
Row 62: *K1, p1, rep from * to end.
Rep row 62 nine more times.
Bind off knitwise.

FINISHING
Sew back seam neatly.
Make 4 small pom-poms using M and C yarn.
Attach a short length of C to one pom-pom and thread through leg warmer, immediately below rib section. Attach other pom-pom to end of this yarn. Embellish second legwarmer in the same way.

SIZE

16½in long

YARN SUGGESTION

3 1¾oz balls of bulky-weight yarn (such as Rowan Little Big Wool) in main color (M)
1 1¾oz ball of bulky-weight yarn (such as Rowan Little Big Wool) in contrast color (C)

NEEDLES

Pair of US 11 knitting needles
Knitter's sewing needle

GAUGE

18 stitches and 12 rows to 4in square over stockinette stitch using US 11 needles.

ABBREVIATIONS

See page 120.

Note: work pattern using the Fair Isle technique, stranding yarn not in use loosely across the back.

in the middle

tweed bag

This bag is designed to hold your day-to-day essentials: diary, wallet, phone, keys, make-up bag, and a wooly hat. I love the tweedy yarn mixed with the wooden handles as it seems such a natural marriage. There are lots of similar handles out there, so don't worry if you can't find exactly the same ones. You can also line the bag with a favorite fabric to help keep the shape.

SIZE

Approximately 13 x 13in

YARN SUGGESTION

2 3½oz hanks of bulky-weight yarn (such as Debbie Bliss Donegal Tweed Chunky

NEEDLES

Pair of US 10½ knitting needles
Knitter's sewing needle

OTHER MATERIALS

2 wooden handles

GAUGE

12 stitches and 19 rows to 4in square over stockinette stitch using US 10½ needles.

ABBREVIATIONS

See page 120.

PATTERN

BACK AND FRONT
(both alike)
Cast on 42 sts.
Row 1: K2, *p2, k2, rep from * to end.
Row 2: P2, *k2, p2, rep from * to end.
Rep the last 2 rows three more times.**
Beg with a knit row, cont in st st.
Work 20 rows.
Rep from ** to ** once more.
Beg with a knit row cont in st st.
Work 8 rows.
Mark each end of last row with a contrast thread.
Dec row: K2, skpo, k to last 4 sts, k2tog, k2.
Next row: K2, p to the last 2 sts, k2.
Rep the last 2 rows five more times.
Rep from ** to ** once more.
Bind off.

HANDLE STRAPS
(make 4)
Cast on 6 sts.
Work 2 rows st st.
Bind off.

FINISHING
Join bottom and side seams as far as contrast threads. Thread handle straps through holes on handles and sew to top of bag.

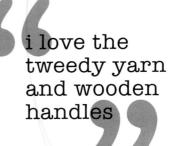

i love the tweedy yarn and wooden handles

gold clutch bag

Whoever thought a knitted bag could be so chic! Everything you need for an evening out will fit inside this little clutch. It would also look good with an over-the-shoulder strap so it sits under the arm, or you could sling it across your body 80s-style. I suggest a 24in strap if you want it to sit snugly under your arm, or 43in for the longer length.

PATTERN

BAG
Cast on 78 sts.
Row 1 (RS): *K2, p2, rep from * to last 2 sts, k2.
Row 2: *P2, k2, rep from * to last 2 sts, p2.
Rep rows 1–2 until work measures 6in from cast on edge, ending with a WS row.
First fold line
Next row: Knit.
Next row: Purl.
Next row: Knit.
Bag back
Next row: *P2, k2, rep from * eight times, p14, **k2, p2, rep from ** to end.
Next row: *K2, p2, rep from * eight times, k14, **p2, k2, rep from ** to end.
Rep last two rows until work measures 6in from first fold line, ending with a RS row.
Second fold line
Next row: Purl.
Next row: Knit.
Next row: Purl.
Front flap
Next row: *K2, p2, rep from * eight times, k14, **p2, k2, rep from ** to end.
Next row: *P2, k2, rep from * eight times, p14, **k2, p2, rep from ** to end.
Rep last two rows six more times.
Next row: *K2, p2, rep from * eight

times, k14, **p2, k2, rep from ** to end.
Shape corners
Keeping st st panel as set, work as folls:
Next row: P2, k2tog, work to last 4 sts, p2togtbl, k2.
Next row: K2, p2tog, work to last 4 sts, k2togtbl, p2.
Rep last two rows once more.
Bind off in patt.

LOOP
Work 13-in length of French knitting (see page 96.)

FINISHING
WS facing, fold bag at first fold line and sew up side seams.
Fold loop in half and sew to top of left-hand side seam.
If you want to make a closure for the bag, make a strap and buckle following the pattern for Gold Belt (see page 40.) Make the strap long enough to go around the bag and sew it to the center back of the bag.

SIZE

9½ x 6in

YARN SUGGESTION

4 ¾oz balls of lurex yarn (such as Arista Crochet yarn)

NEEDLES

Pair of US 2 knitting needles
Knitter's sewing needle

GAUGE

32 stitches and 27 rows to 4in square over 2x2 rib using 2 ends of yarn and US 2 needles.

ABBREVIATIONS

See page 120.

Note: use 2 ends of yarn throughout.

cute bow

This little bow is quick to knit and can be used to spice up plain knitwear or to add a sweet touch to any other outfit, including one for a fashionable pooch. You only need a small amount of yarn and it's very quick to knit, so make lots in different colors.

PATTERN

MAIN PIECE
Cast on 11 sts.
Row 1: Knit.
Row 2: K1, p to last st, k1.
Row 3: K1, [m1, k2] five times. *16 sts*
**Row 4: K1, p to last st, k1.
Row 5: Knit.
Row 6: K1, p to last st, k1.
Rows 7–22: Rep the last 2 rows eight more times.
Row 23: K1, [k2 tog, k1] five times. *11 sts*
Row 24: K1, p to last st, k1.
Row 25: Knit.
Row 26: K1, p to last st, k1.**
Row 27: K1, [m1, k2] five times. *16 sts*
Rep from ** to ** once more.
Bind off.

CENTER PIECE
Cast on 4 sts.
Row 1: Knit.
Row 2: K1, p to last st, k1.
Rep the last 2 rows until piece measures 2½in, ending with a row 2.
Bind off.

FINISHING
Sew cast on and bound off edges of main piece together. Place seam to center back of main piece. Wrap center piece around middle of main piece, sew cast on and bound off edges together.

SIZE

2⅝in wide by 3in long

YARN SUGGESTION

Small amount of sport-weight yarn or lurex yarn

NEEDLES

Pair of US 3 knitting needles
Knitter's sewing needle

GAUGE

24 stitches and 32 rows to 4in square over stockinette stitch using US 3 needles.

ABBREVIATIONS

See page 120.

"add a cute touch to a favorite outfit with this knitted bow"

ribbed belt with covered buckle

This knitted belt can be worn on your waist over a dress or through your jeans' belt loops on your hips. It's easy to lengthen or shorten it to fit your size. I've given you pattern variations to widen the belt to suit different buckle widths.

SIZE

Approximately 1¼(1½:2)in wide
To fit any waist measurement

YARN SUGGESTION

2 ¾oz balls of lurex yarn
(such as Arista Crochet yarn)

NEEDLES

Pair of US 2 knitting needles
Knitter's sewing needle

OTHER MATERIALS

Buckle without tongue, large enough to fit chosen belt width
Knitter's sewing needle

GAUGE

It is not necessary to achieve a specific gauge for this project.

ABBREVIATIONS

See page 120.

PATTERN

BUCKLE COVERING
Using a single end of yarn, cast on 6 sts.
Work in st st until the strip of knitted fabric, when slightly stretched, is long enough to wrap around the outside of the buckle.
Right-sides facing, fold strip in half lengthwise, aligning cast on edge with sts on needle.
Knit first st on right-hand needle together with first st on cast on edge.
Knit second st on right-hand needle together with second st on cast on edge. Pass first st on left-hand needle over second st. Cont in this way until all 6 sts are bound off. Fasten off.
Slip loop of knitted fabric around buckle. Stitch row ends neatly together, twisting them so that the seam is on the inside of the buckle.

BELT
Using a single end of yarn, cast on 14(18:22) sts.
Work in st st until until work measures 2½in from cast on, ending with a purl row.
Right side up, wrap knitted fabric around central bar of buckle.
Knit first st on right-hand needle together with first st on cast on edge. Cont until all cast on sts

have been knitted together with sts on needle.
Next row (WS): Purl.
Join in end of yarn from second ball.
Next row: *K2, p2, rep from * to last 2 sts, k2.
Next row: P2, k2, rep from * to last 2 sts, p2.
Rep these last 2 rows until work measures waist measurement plus 8in (or desired length), ending with a WS row.
Shape end
1¼in-wide belt
**Next row: K2, p2, k2, p2tog, k2, p2, k2. *13 sts*
Next row: P2, k2, p2tog, k1, p2togtbl, k2, p2. *11 sts*
Next row: K2, p1, p2tog, p1, p2tog tbl, p1, k2. *9 sts*
Next row: P2, k2togtbl, k1, k2tog, p2. *7 sts*
Next row: K2, sl 1, p2tog, psso, k2. *5 sts*
Next row: P1, p3tog, P1. *3 sts*
Next row: Sl 1, k2tog, psso. *1 st*
Fasten off.**
1½in-wide belt
***Next row: K2, p2, k2, p1, p2tog twice, p1, k2, p2, k2. *16 sts*
Next row: P2, k2, p2, k2togtbl, k2tog, p2, k2, p2. *14 sts*
Work from ** to ** of 1¼in-wide belt.

> "a gold belt is essential in any cool wardrobe"

2in-wide belt

Next row: K2, p2, k2, p2, k1, k2togtbl, k2tog, k1, p2, k2, p2, k2. *20 sts*

Next row: P2, k2, p2, k2, p2tog twice, k2, p2, k2, p2. *18 sts*

Work as 1½in-wide belt from *** to end.

BELT LOOP

Using a single end of yarn, cast on 10 sts.

Work in st st until the knitted fabric measures twice the width of the belt, plus ¼in.

Bind off.

FINISHING

Wrong-sides facing, fold the belt loop in half lengthwise and sew row edges together. Sew cast on and bound off ends together, positioning row seam inside.

Slip loop onto belt with seam at center back. Slide to approximately 4in from the buckle and stitch in place at center back.

beehive scarf

The chunky texture of this scarf means you'll never be cold, even in the most bitter winter wind, and I've made the scarf to a big size to make sure you're super-cozy. A wider version of the same stitch pattern would even make a great wrap.

PATTERN

Cast on 25 sts.

Row 1: Knit.

Row 2: Knit to last st, pick up loop lying between needles and place this loop on right needle (this loop does NOT count as a st), slip last st knitwise.

Row 3: K tog the first st and the picked-up loop, knit to last st, pick up loop lying between needles and place this loop on right needle (this loop does NOT count as a st), slip last st knitwise.

Rows 4–6: As row 3.

Keeping first and last 3 sts correct as set by first 6 rows, now work center 19 sts in beehive patt as folls:

Row 1: Patt 3 sts, [sl 1, k3] four times, sl 1, k2, patt 3 sts.

Row 2: Patt 3 sts, p2, sl 1, [p3, sl 1] four times, patt 3 sts.

Rows 3–4: Patt 3 sts, p19, patt 3 sts.

Row 5: Patt 3 sts, k2, sl 1, [k3, sl 1] four times, patt 3 sts.

Row 6: Patt 3 sts, [sl 1, p3] four times, sl 1, p2, patt 3 sts.

Rows 7–8: Patt 3 sts, p19, patt 3 sts.

These 8 rows form beehive patt.

Cont as set until scarf measures approximately 70in, ending after beehive patt row 3 or 7.

Next row: K tog the first st and the picked-up loop, knit to last st, pick up loop lying between needles and place this loop on right needle (this loop does NOT count as a st), slip last st knitwise.

Rep this row four more times.

Bind off.

FINISHING

Cut 44 lengths of yarn, each 16in long, and knot each length through a cast on or bound off stitch to form fringe.

SIZE

7½in wide and 70in long, excluding fringe

YARN SUGGESTION

6 1¾oz balls of bulky-weight yarn (such as Rowan Little Big Wool)

NEEDLES

Pair of US 13 knitting needles

GAUGE

13 stitches and 20 rows to 4in square over beehive patt using US 13 needles.

ABBREVIATIONS

See page 120.

simple snood

This snood is extremely easy and very quick to make. You don't need much yarn and you could probably knit it up in an evening if you put your mind to it. Keep it tucked in your handbag and bring it out when you need that little extra bit of warmth: you can even wear it as an earwarmer or headband. However you wear it, it will be especially good for ski bunnies, as it will keep you warm but won't get in the way of any strenuous physical activity.

SIZE

Approximately 22in diameter and 9in deep

YARN SUGGESTION

2 1¾oz balls of bulky-weight yarn (such as Jaeger Extra Fine Merino Chunky)

NEEDLES

Set of 4 double-pointed US 10 knitting needles
Round marker
Knitter's sewing needle

GAUGE

13.5 stitches and 20 rows to 4in square over lace patt using US 10 needles.

ABBREVIATIONS

See page 120.

PATTERN

SNOOD
Cast on 75 sts and distribute these 75 sts evenly over 3 needles (25 sts on each needle) and place marker.
Using 4th needle, work in rounds as folls:
Rounds 1–2: Knit.
Round 3: *K3, yo, k2tog, rep from * to end.
Rep these 3 rounds thirteen more times, then rounds 1 and 2 again.
Bind off.

FINISHING
Darn in ends neatly, then press carefully.

this snood will keep the most active ski bunny super-cozy

lacy shawl

You can just imagine your great-great-grandmother getting into her horse-drawn carriage wearing a voluminous dress with a lovely handmade shawl just like this one to cover her shoulders. Today, wear it around your shoulders like a scarf, or as a cover-up on summer evenings. The long fingerless gloves on page 18 are the perfect accompaniment to this shawl.

PATTERN

Lace panel
Worked over 15 sts.
Row 1: P1, yo, k1, yo, s1 1, k2tog, psso, k9, p1.
Row 2 and every foll alt row: K1, p13, k1.
Row 3: P1, [k1, yo] twice, k1, sl 1, k2tog, psso, k7, p1.
Row 5: P1, k2, yo, k1, yo, k2, sl 1, k2tog, psso, k5, p1.
Row 7: P1, k3, yo, k1, yo, k3, sl 1, k2tog, psso, k3, p1.
Row 9: P1, k9, k3tog, yo, k1, yo, p1.
Row 11: P1, k7, k3tog, [k1, yo] twice, k1, p1.
Row 13: P1, k5, k3tog, k2, yo, k1, yo, k2, p1.
Row 15: P1, k3, k3tog, k3, yo, k1, yo, k3, p1.
Row 16: As row 2.
These 16 rows form lace panel and are repeated.

SHAWL

Using 2 strands of yarn held together, cast on 21 sts.
Row 1: K5, p2, k13, inc purlwise in last st. 22 sts
Row 2: Inc in first st, k1, p13, k2, p4, pick up loop lying between needles and place this loop onto right-hand needle (this loop does NOT count as a st), slip last st purlwise. 23 sts
Row 3: K tog the slipped st and the picked-up loop, k4, p1, work next 15 sts as row 1 of lace panel, p1, k1.
Last 2 rows set position of lace panel and form slip st edging at straight (unshaped) row end edge.
Keeping patt correct as now set, cont as folls:
Row 4: Inc in first st, k1, patt to end. 24 sts
Row 5: Patt 21 sts, p1, k2.
Row 6: Inc in first st, p1, k1, patt to end. 25 sts
Row 7: Patt 21 sts, p1, k3.
Cont in this way, inc 1 st at beg of next and 4 foll alt rows, taking inc sts into st st. 30 sts
Inc 1 st at end (shaped edge) of next row. 31 sts
Inc 1 st at beg of next and foll 7 alt rows, taking inc sts into st st. 39 sts
Row 33: Patt 6 sts, (work next 15 sts as lace panel) twice, p2, inc in last st. 40 sts
**Inc 1 st at beg of next and foll 7 alt rows, taking inc sts into st st. 48 sts
Inc 1 st at end (shaped edge) of next row. 49 sts
Rep from ** ten more times, taking inc

SIZE

Approximately 63in along longest edge and approximately 25in wide.

YARN SUGGESTION

8 ¾oz balls of fine kid mohair yarn (such as Rowan Kidsilk Haze)

NEEDLES

Pair of US 6 knitting needles
Knitter's sewing needle

GAUGE

24 stitches and 28 rows to 4in square over stockinette stitch using 2 strands of yarn held together and US 6 needles.

ABBREVIATIONS

See page 120.

sts into st st until there are sufficient to work in lace panel patt. *139 sts*

Inc 1 st at beg of next row. *140 sts*

Work should now be 9 lace panels wide plus edge sts at straight edge, and row 16 of 13th rep of first lace panel should now have been completed.

***Work 1 row.

Keeping patt correct, dec 1 st at shaped edge of next and foll 6 alt rows, then on foll 2 rows. *131 sts*

Rep from *** twelve more times. *23 sts*

Row 16 of 26th rep of lace panel should now have been completed.

Bind off.

FRILL

(make 4)

Cast on 226 sts very loosely using 2 strands of yarn held together.

Row 1: Knit.

Row 2: *K1, insert right needle point into st directly below next st on left needle and k this st, letting st above slip off left needle at same time, rep from * to last 2 sts, k2.

Rep row 2 until Frill measures 2½in.

Next row: *K2tog, rep from * to end. *113 sts*

Starting with a purl row, work in st st for 3 rows.

Bind off loosely.

FINISHING

Join ends of Frills to make one long strip, then sew bound off edge of Frills to shaped row end edge of Shawl.

"a glamourous cover-up for cool summer evenings"

head first

bow beanie

This cute style of hat is ever-popular and I really wanted to include a version everyone can make. I like it in girly colors or muted vintage combinations and the velvet bow can be either a contrasting or a matching color. If you can find it, use stretchy velvet ribbon, though plain velvet will do the job well. Knit a pair of either the long or short fingerless gloves on pages 10–13 to go with your beanie to make a stylish set.

SIZE

To fit average-size adult head

YARN SUGGESTION

1 1¾oz ball of bulky-weight yarn (such as Rowan Little Big Wool) in main color (M)
1 1¾oz ball of bulky-weight yarn (such as Rowan Little Big Wool) in contrast color (C)

NEEDLES

Pair of US 11 knitting needles
Knitter's sewing needle

OTHER MATERIALS

43in of 1-in wide stretchy velvet ribbon

GAUGE

12 stitches and 18 rows to 4in square over stockinette stitch using US 11 needles.

ABBREVIATIONS

See page 120.

PATTERN

Using C, cast on 53 sts.
Row 1 (RS): *K1, p1, rep from * to last st, k1.
Rep row 1 seven more times.
Change to M.
Row 9 (eyelet row): K1, *yo, k2tog, rep from * to end.
Row 10: Purl.
Row 11: Knit
Rep rows 10–11 seven more times.
Rep row 10 once more.
Shape crown
Row 27: K3, *k2tog, k3, rep from * to end. *43 sts*
Row 20 and foll 2 alt rows: Purl.
Row 21: K2, *k2tog, k2, rep from * to last st, k1. *33 sts*
Row 23: *K2tog, k1, rep from * to end. *22 sts*
Row 25: *K2tog, rep from * to end. *11 sts*
Row 26: *P2tog, rep from * to last st, p1. *6 sts*
Break yarn, thread through rem sts, pull up tight and secure.

FINISHING
Sew seam neatly.
With the crown of the beanie toward you, following chart on page 13 and main photograph, Swiss-darn fleur-de-lys patterns onto M part of beanie, using C.
Thread ribbon through eyelets and tie in bow on one side of beanie.

cloche hat

Whether it's keeping cozy on a cold day or covering up on a bad hair day, this dogtooth check hat is the perfect answer. Just pull it on and you'll be instantly warm and neat. Wear it as it comes or pin up one side with a big kilt pin for a jaunty look.

PATTERN

HAT
Using A, cast on 66 sts.
Row 1: Knit.
Row 2: Purl.
Row 3: Knit.
Row 4: Knit.
Change to B
Row 5: K2, *sl 1, K3, rep from * to end.
Row 6: P3, *sl 1, p3, rep from * to last 3 sts, sl 1, p2.
Row 7: As row 5
Row 8: Knit.
Change to A.
Row 9: K4, *sl 1, k3, rep from * to last 2 sts, sl 1, k1.
Row 10: P1, *. sl 1, p3, rep from * to last st, p1.
Row 11: As row 9
Row 12: Knit.
Rep rows 5–12 twice more, then rep rows 5–6 again.
Shape crown
Cont in B.
Row 31: K2, *k2tog, k2, rep from * to end. *50 sts*
Row 32: P1, *p2tog, p1, rep from * to last st, p1. *34 sts*
Row 33: *K2tog, rep from * to end. *17 sts*
Row 34: *P2tog, rep from * to last st, p1. *9 sts*
Break yarn, thread through rem sts and pull up tight.

BRIM
Using B, cast on 10sts.
Row 1: Knit.
Row 2: Knit.
Row 3: K7, turn, k to end.
Row 4: Knit across all sts.
Rep rows 2–4 until when slightly stretched shorter edge of brim fits around cast on edge of hat.
Bind off.

FINISHING
Sew back seam of hat. Sew shorter edge of brim to cast on edge of hat.

SIZE

To fit average-size adult head

YARN SUGGESTION

1 1¾oz ball of bulky-weight yarn (such as Rowan Little Big Wool) in white (A)
2 1¾oz balls of bulky-weight yarn (such as Rowan Little Big Wool) in black (B)

NEEDLES

Pair of US 13 knitting needles
Knitter's sewing needle

GAUGE

15 stitches and 23 rows to 4in square over patt using US 13 needles.

ABBREVIATIONS

See page 120.

Note: slip all sts purlwise to avoid twisting them.

sequined earmuffs

Easy and quick to make, these will keep your ears beautifully warm, and they look very cute in girly colors. I've hand-stitched in a lining of thick, felted wool to give the earmuffs extra warmth, but you could also line them with fleece, corduroy, or even a sweet, brushed-cotton print. The sequins have been hand-stitched onto each ear, but the earmuffs would look just as cool with big pom-poms on each ear.

PATTERN

ONE EARMUFF
(make 2)
Cast on 2 sts.
Row 1: Knit.
Row 2: K1, m1, k1.
Row 3: K1, p1, k1.
Row 4: K1, m1, k1, m1, k1.
Row 5: K1, p3, k1.
Row 6: K1, m1, k to last st, m1, k1.
Row 7: K1, p to last st, k1.
Rep rows 6–7 three more times. *13 sts*
Row 14: K1, skpo, k to last 3 sts, k2tog, k1.
Work 3 rows.
Rep the last 4 rows once more.
Rep row 14 once more. *7 sts*
Work 5 rows.
Row 28: K1, skpo, k to last 3 sts, k2tog, k1.
Work 9 rows st st.
Bind off.

FINISHING
Sew bound off edges together. Press earmuffs. Right-side down, lay the knitting on the felt and draw around the knitting with the fabric marker. Cut out the shape. Turning under ¼-in all around and using the sewing needle and matching thread, blanket stitch the felt to the back of the knitting. Following the photograph, sew a spiral of sequins to each earmuff (see page 94), joining them with a line of sequins across the straight section. Sew a length of ribbon to the point of each earmuff.

SIZE

To fit average-size adult head

YARN SUGGESTION

1 1¾oz ball of bulky-weight yarn (such as Rowan Little Big Wool)

NEEDLES

Pair of US 11 knitting needles
Knitter's sewing needle

OTHER MATERIALS

18 x 4in piece of felt
Fabric marker
Scissors
Sewing needle and thread to match yarn
Approximately 100 silver sequins
Pink sewing thread
2 32in lengths of ⅝-in wide pink satin ribbon

GAUGE

12 stitches and 18 rows to 4in square over stockinette stitch using US 11 needles.

ABBREVIATIONS

See page 120.

"knitted in white, this beanie is very demure"

lacy beanie

Knitted in white this beanie is very demure and the scalloped hem makes a nice soft edge to frame the face. I picked a lovely antique-white cotton lace to make into a rosette, which gives the beanie a vintage feel, but it would look fun in a bright color, too.

PATTERN

Using 2 strands of yarn held together, cast on 101 sts.

Knit 1 row.

Now work in lace patt as folls:

Row 1: K2tog, *k3, yo, k1, yo, k3, sl 1, k2tog, psso, rep from * to last 9 sts, k3, yo, k1, yo, k3, sl 1, k1, psso.

Row 2 and every foll alt row: Purl.

Row 3: K2tog, *k2, yo, k3, yo, k2, sl 1, k2tog, psso, rep from * to last 9 sts, k2, yo, k3, yo, k2, sl 1, k1, psso.

Row 5: K2tog, *k1, yo, k5, yo, k1, sl 1, k2tog, psso, rep from * to last 9 sts, k1, yo, k5, yo, k1, sl 1, k1, psso.

Row 7: K2tog, *yo, k7, yo, sl 1, k2tog, psso, rep from * to last 9 sts, yo, k7, yo, sl 1, k1, psso.

Row 8: Purl.

These 8 rows form lace patt.

Rep last 8 rows four more times.

Next row: K1, *k3, k2tog, rep from * to end. *81 sts*

Next row: Purl.

Next row: K1, *k2, k2tog, rep from * to end. *61 sts*

Next row: Purl.

Next row: K1, *k1, k2tog, rep from * to end. *41 sts*

Next row: Purl.

Next row: K1, *k2tog, rep from * to end. *21 sts*

Next row: Purl.

Break yarn and thread through rem 21 sts. Pull up tight and fasten off securely.

FINISHING

Sew back seam. Coil the lace up like a snail, stitching the bottom edge to the back of the previous coil as you go to make a rosette. Stitch the rosette to the side of the beanie.

SIZE

To fit small to medium adult head

YARN SUGGESTION

1 ¾oz ball of fine kid mohair yarn (such as Rowan Kidsilk Haze)

NEEDLES

Pair of US 6 knitting needles

Knitter's sewing needle

OTHER MATERIALS

28in of ½-in wide lace

Sewing needle and thread

GAUGE

23 stitches and 32 rows to 4in square over lace patt using 2 strands of yarn held together and US 6 needles.

ABBREVIATIONS

See page 120.

embellished beret

Berets are a classic hat style and will give any outfit instant chic. If you only knit one hat, this beret is the one to make. Feel free to get creative and put your own stamp on your berets by adding buttons or bows instead of vintage lace. Berets don't have to be worn at a jaunty angle, Parisian-artist-style: they're very cute pulled down to cover your ears or worn almost vertically behind the ears to show your hairline.

SIZE

To fit average-size adult head

YARN SUGGESTION

2 1¾oz balls of bulky-weight yarn (such as Rowan Little Big Wool)

NEEDLES

Pair of US 11 knitting needles
Knitter's sewing needle

OTHER MATERIALS

Pieces of vintage lace
Sewing needle and thread

GAUGE

12 stitches and 18 rows to 4in square over stockinette stitch using US 11 needles.

ABBREVIATIONS

See page 120.

PATTERN

Cast on 54 sts.
Row 1: *K1, p1, rep from * to end.
Rep row 1 twice more.
Row 4 (RS): *K1, inc, rep from * to end. *81 sts*
Row 5: Purl.
Row 6: K4, *inc, k7, rep from * to last 5 sts, inc, k4. *91 sts*
Row 7 and foll 2 alt rows: Purl.
Row 8: K5, *inc, k8, rep from * to last 5 sts, inc, k4. *101 sts*
Row 10: K6, *inc, k9, rep from * to last 5 sts, inc, k4. *111 sts*
Row 12: K7, *inc, k10, rep from * to last 5 sts, inc, k4. *121 sts*
Row 13: Purl.
Row 14: Knit.
Row 15: Purl.
Rep rows 14–15 twice more.
Shape crown
Row 20: K7, *k2tog, k10, rep from * to last 6 sts, k2tog, k4. *111 sts*
Row 21 and foll 8 alt rows: Purl.
Row 22: K6, *k2tog, k9, rep from * to last 6 sts, k2tog, k4. *101 sts*
Row 24: K5, *k2tog, k8, rep from * to last 6 sts, k2tog, k4. *91 sts*
Row 26: K4, *k2tog, k7, rep from * to last 6 sts, k2tog, k4. *81 sts*
Row 28: K3, *k2tog, k6, rep from * to last 6 sts, k2tog, k4. *71 sts*
Row 30: K2, *k2tog, k5, rep from * to last 6 sts, k2tog, k4. *61 sts*
Row 32: K1, *k2tog, k4, rep from * to last 6 sts, k2tog, k4. *51 sts*
Row 34: *K2tog, k3, rep from * to last 6 sts, k2tog, k4. *41 sts*
Row 36: *K2, k2tog, rep from * to last st, k1. *31 sts*
Row 38: *K1, k2tog, rep from * to last st, k1. *21 sts*
Row 39: *P2tog, rep from * to last st, p1. *11 sts*
Break yarn, thread through rem 11 sts, pull up tightly and secure.

FINISHING

Sew seam neatly. Position the pieces of lace on your beret and when you are happy with the look, sew them in place (see page 91.)

hat with cable earflaps

Made with two different yarn weights, you might at first find this hat mildly challenging to knit, but I'm sure you'll agree that the chunkier yarn over the ears looks great and it will keep your ears extra-cozy. I've used Rowan Big Wool for the cable section and Little Big Wool for the main part of the hat, but the same size needles throughout, so you will have a looser knit in the main section. In neutral colors like cream and caramel you'll be able to wear this hat with any casual outfit, and in brighter colors it will have a vibrant, younger look. I've made a two-color cord with pom-poms at the ends, which you can tie under your chin in a bow or leave hanging down.

SIZE

To fit average-size adult head

YARN SUGGESTION

1 3½oz ball of extra-bulky-weight yarn (such as Rowan Big Wool)
2 1¾oz balls of bulky-weight yarn (such as Rowan Little Big Wool)

NEEDLES

Pair of US 11 knitting needles
Cable needle
Knitter's sewing needle

GAUGE

12 stitches and 18 rows to 4in square over stockinette stitch using bulky-weight yarn and US 11 needles.

ABBREVIATIONS

See page 120.

PATTERN

LEFT EARFLAP
Using C, cast on 2 sts.
Row 1 (RS): Inc in each st. *4 sts*
Row 2: Purl.
Row 3: K1, M1, k2, M1, k1. *6 sts*
Row 4: Purl.
Join in M.
Row 5: K1M, M1C, k4C, M1C, k1M. *8 sts*
Row 6: P1M, p6C, p1M.
Row 7: K1M, M1M, k6C, M1M, k1M. *10 sts*
Row 8: P2M, p6C, p2M.
Row 9: K1M, M1M, k1M, C6FC, k1M, M1M, k1M. *12 sts*
Row 10: P3M, p6C, p3M.
Row 11: K1M, M1M, k2M, k6C, k2M, M1M, k1M. *14 sts*
Row 12: P4M, p6C, p4M.
Row 13: K1M, M1M, k3M, k6C, k3M, M1M, k1M. *16 sts*
Row 14: P5M, p6C, p5M.
Row 15: K1M, M1M, k4M, k6C, k4M, M1M, k1M. *18 sts*
Row 16: P6M, p6C, p6M.
Row 17: K1M, M1M, k5M, C6FC, k5M, M1M, k1M. *20 sts*
Row 18: P7M, p6C, p7M.
Break M, leaving a 6in tail.

Break C, leaving a 3-yd length of yarn.
Put all sts on a holder.

RIGHT EARFLAP
Work as for Left Earflap, substituting C6B for C6F.

HAT
Using M, cast on 7 sts, knit 20 sts of Left Earflap from holder knitting central 6 sts using tail of C, using M, cast on 16 sts, knit 20 sts of Right Earlap from holder knitting central 6 sts using tail of C, using M, cast on 7 sts. *70 sts*
Keeping bands of 6 sts in C as set, work as folls:
Next row: Purl.
Next row: Knit.
Rep these rows once more.
Next row: Purl.
Next row: K14, C6F, k30, C6B, k14.
**Next row: Purl.
Next row: Knit.
Rep these rows twice more.
Next row: Purl.
Next row: K14, C6F, k30, C6B, k14.**
Rep from ** to ** once more.
Next row: Purl.
Shape crown
Next row: K1, k2tog, k6, k2tog, k3, k6 (in C), k5, k2tog, k6, k2tog, skpo, k6, skpo, k5, k6 (in C), k3, skpo, k6, skpo, k1. *62 sts*
Next and foll 2 alt rows: Purl.
Next row: K1, k2tog, k4, k2tog, k3, slip next 3 C sts onto cable needle and hold at front of work, knit each st on cable needle together with next C st on left-hand needle to make 3 sts in C in total, k4, k2tog, k5, k2tog, skpo, k5, skpo, k4, slip next 3 C sts onto cable needle and hold at back of work, knit each st on cable needle together with next C st on left-hand needle to make 3 sts in C in total, k3, skpo, k4, skpo, k1. *48 sts*
Next row: K1, k2tog, k2, k2tog, k1, k2tog, k3 (in C), skpo, k1, k2tog, k4, k2tog, skpo, k4, skpo, k1, k2tog, k3 (in C), skpo, k1, skpo, k2, skpo, k1. *36 sts*

Next row: K1, [k2tog] three times, slip next 2 sts (in C), k1 (in C), pass both slipped sts over knitted st, [k2tog] four times, [skpo] four times, k3tog (in C), [skpo] three times, k1. *18 sts*
Next row: [P2tog] twice, k1 (in C), [p2tog] four times, k1 (in C), [p2tog] twice. *10 sts*
Break M. Thread end of M through all 10 sts and pull up tight.

FINISHING
Weave in all ends. Sew back seam neatly.
Using 1 strand each of M and C, make two 12-in long lengths of twisted cord. Using M and C, make two pom-poms. Tie a knot 2in from one end of each length of cord and untwist the two strands of yarn below it. Tie these strands around the middle of a pom-pom. Knot the other ends of the cords through the cast on sts of the earflaps.

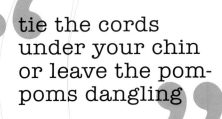

tie the cords under your chin or leave the pom- poms dangling

home comforts

covered coat hanger

These coat hangers are perfect for those troublesome dresses that keep falling down in your wardrobe and they will also protect your clothes from shoulder dents as the corners are soft and rounded. Your clothes will look gorgeous hung on different-colored covered hangers all in a row, and you will be able to use up all those leftovers of sport-weight yarn. A covered coat hanger will also make a great fun gift.

SIZE

Adjustable to fit any length of coat hanger

YARN SUGGESTION

1 1¾oz ball of sport-weight yarn (such as Rowan Pure Wool DK)

NEEDLES

Pair of US 6 knitting needles
Knitter's sewing needle

OTHER MATERIALS

2–4 tiny artificial flowers
Length of narrow satin ribbon

GAUGE

22 stitches and 30 rows to 4in square over stockinette stitch using US 6 needles.

ABBREVIATIONS

See page 120.

PATTERN

MAIN SECTION
Cast on 11 sts.
Row 1: Knit.
Rep this row until this strip, slightly stretched, is same length as coat hanger.
Bind off.

HOOK COVER
Cast on 23 sts.
Row 1: Knit.
Rep this row five more times.
Bind off.

FINISHING
Gently push hook through center of main section, then wrap main section around body of coat hanger. Sew row end edges together, gathering cast on and bound off edges at ends of hanger. Join cast on and bound off edges of hook cover and close one end. Slip hook cover over coat hanger hook, and sew end of cover to main section at base of hook. Tie ribbon in a bow around base of hook and attach flowers as in photograph.

"your clothes will look gorgeous on these hangers"

egg cozies

Egg cozies are another perfect way to use up any leftover sport-weight yarn and are a great starter project for beginners. The pattern is for a striped cozy—just change the colors and row counts as you wish. Buttons or beads will look great as eyes and all manner of ribbons and other trims could be used for the hair; you could even add some earrings. Imagine the great hairstyles you could create—plaits anyone?

PATTERN

Using A, cast on 35 sts.
Rows 1–2: Knit in A.
Join in B.
Rows 3–4: Knit in B.
Rows 5–6: Knit in A.
Row 7: Knit in B.
Row 8: Purl in B.
Row 9: Knit in A.
Row 10: Purl in A.
Rows 7–10 form stripe patt.
Work in stripe patt for another 6 rows, ending after 2 rows B.
Keeping stripes correct as set, shape top of egg cozy as folls:
Row 17: [K5, k2tog] five times. *30 sts*
Work 1 row.
Row 19: [K4, k2tog] five times. *25 sts*
Work 1 row.
Row 21: [K3, k2tog] five times. *20 sts*
Work 1 row.
Row 23: [K2, k2tog] five times. *15 sts*
Work 1 row.
Row 25: [K1, k2tog] five times. *10 sts*
Work 1 row.
Break yarn and thread through rem 10 sts. Pull up tight and fasten off securely.

FINISHING

Sew back seam. Using photograph as a guide, embroider mouth in backstitch using red yarn and attach eyes. Cut short lengths of peach yarn and knot through top to form hair, unraveling strands to create tufted effect. Using A, make a loop on top of egg cozy, behind hair, by working buttonhole stitch over several strands of yarn.

SIZE

5¾in diameter and 3in tall, excluding hair

YARN SUGGESTION

Oddments of sport-weight yarn (such as Rowan Scottish Tweed DK) in (A) and (B)

NEEDLES

Pair of US 5 knitting needles
Knitter's sewing needle

OTHER MATERIALS

Small amount of fine red yarn (for mouth) and thick peach yarn (for hair)
2 tiny toy eyes

GAUGE

24 stitches and 32 rows to 4in square over stockinette stitch using US 5 needles.

ABBREVIATIONS

See page 120.

corset cushion

Great on your sofa as well as on your bed, this cushion is lovely in rich boudoir colors, such as deep red and pink or black and white, as well as the burgundy and teal used here. To set off the ribbon I've hand-stitched around the buttonholes.

PATTERN

MAIN COVER
Using the thumb method and M, cast on 59 sts.
Row 1 (RS): *K1, p1, rep from * to last st, k1.
This row establishes seed stitch.
Rep row 1 twice more.
Row 4: Purl.
Row 5: K6, *yo, k2tog, k3, rep from * to last 3 sts, k3.
Row 6: Purl.
Work 10 rows in seed stitch.
Row 17: Seed 20, k19, starting with a purl st, seed 20.
Row 18: Seed 19, p21, starting with a knit st, seed 19.
Row 19: Seed 18, k23, starting with a purl st, seed 18.
Row 20: Seed 17, p25, starting with a knit st, seed 17.
Row 21: Seed 16, k27, starting with a purl st, seed 16.
Row 22: Seed 15, p29, starting with a knit st, seed 15.
Row 23: Seed 14, k31, starting with a purl st, seed 14.
Row 24: Seed 13, p33, starting with a knit st, seed 13.
Row 25: Seed 12, k35, starting with a purl st, seed 12.
Row 26: Seed 11, p37, starting with a knit st, seed 11.
Row 27: Seed 10, k39, starting with a purl st, seed 10.
Row 28: Seed 9, p41, starting with a knit st, seed 9.

Row 29: Knit.
Row 30: Purl.
Rep rows 29–30 thirty-four more times.
Row 99: Knit.
Row 100: Seed 9, p41, starting with a knit st, seed 9.
Row 101: Seed 10, k39, starting with a purl st, seed 10.
Row 102: Seed 11, p37, starting with a knit st, seed 11.
Row 103: Seed 12, k35, starting with a purl st, seed 12.
Row 104: Seed 13, p33, starting with a knit st, seed 13.
Row 105: Seed 14, k31, starting with a purl st, seed 14.
Row 106: Seed 15, p29, starting with a knit st, seed 15.
Row 107: Seed 16, k27, starting with a purl st, seed 16.
Row 108: Seed 17, p25, starting with a knit st, seed 17.
Row 109: Seed 18, k23, starting with a purl st, seed 18.
Row 110: Seed 19, p21, starting with a knit st, seed 19.
Row 111: Seed 20, k19, starting with a purl st, seed 20.
Work 10 rows in seed stitch.
Row 122: Purl.
Row 123: K6, *yo, k2tog, k3, rep from * to last 3 sts, k3.
Row 124: Purl.
Work 3 rows in seed stitch.
Bind off in seed.

SIZE
Approximately 16 x 12in

YARN SUGGESTION
4 1¾oz balls of bulky-weight yarn (such as Debbie Bliss Cashmerino Chunky) in main color (M)
1 1¾oz ball of bulky-weight yarn (such as Debbie Bliss Cashmerino Chunky) in contrast color (C)

NEEDLES
Pair of US 10 knitting needles
Knitter's sewing needle

OTHER MATERIALS
90in of ⅝-in wide ribbon

GAUGE
15 stitches and 22 rows to 4in square over stockinette stitch using US 10 needles.

ABBREVIATIONS
See page 120.

INSERT PANEL

Using the cable method and C, cast on 27 sts.

Row 1: Knit.

Row 2: Purl.

Rep rows 1–2 until work measures same as bound off edge of Main Cover.

Bind off.

EMBROIDERY

Split a length of C to make two lengths, each of 2 plies of yarn. Thread a knitter's sewing needle with one length. Using overcasting stitch, embroider around each buttonhole, stitching over one strand of the yarn (see page 94.)

FINISHING

Right side down, lay main cover flat. Fold the cast on and bound off edges over and position them so that there is a 2in gap down the center. Pin in place. Using mattress stitch, sew the row ends together top and bottom. Position the insert panel centrally, laying it under the cast on and bound off edges of the cover. Using mattress stitch, sew the top and bottom to the row ends of the back section of the cover in the gap between the cast on and bound off edges. Turn the cover inside out and slipstitch the unsewn sections of the top and bottom of the insert to the inside of the seams. Slip the cushion into the cover and lace it up with the ribbon through the buttonholes.

cool clothes

tube top and mini skirt

This is such a versatile item that I really wanted to show it worn both ways. As a tube top it's almost corset-like; the diamanté buttons give added drama. As a tube skirt it's very 80's, especially with the racer stripes down the sides. If anyone dares to make it in fluoro colors, please send me a picture as I think it will look very cool. The 2x2 rib makes it extra-stretchy to hug the figure perfectly. To alter the size, cast on more or fewer stitches for the front and back panels.

SIZE

Actual measurements
Bust 29in (unstretched)
Length 15in

YARN SUGGESTION

3 1¾oz balls of sport-weight yarn
(such as Rowan Pure Wool DK)
in main color (M)

1 1¾oz ball of sport-weight yarn
(such as Rowan Pure Wool DK)
in contrast color (C)

NEEDLES

Pair of US 6 knitting needles
Circular US 6 24-in long
knitting needle
Stitch holders
Knitter's sewing needle

OTHER MATERIALS

Four buttons
59in of ¼-in wide ribbon

GAUGE

22 stitches and 30 rows to 4in
square over stockinette stitch
using US 6 needles.

ABBREVIATIONS

See page 120.

PATTERN

BACK
With US 6 needles and M, cast on 72 sts.
Row 1: K3, *p2, k2, rep from * to last 5 sts, p2, k3.
Row 2: P3, *k2, p2, rep from * to last 5 sts, k2, p3.
These 2 rows form rib.
Work a further 118 rows, dec 1 st at each end of last row. *70 sts*
Leave these sts on a holder.

FRONT
With US 6 needles and M, cast on 72 sts.
Work 90 rows in rib as given for Back.
Front opening
Row 1: Rib 34, turn and work on these sts for first side of front opening.
Work a further 29 rows, dec 1 st at end of last row. *33 sts*
Leave these sts on a holder.
With right side facing, rejoin yarn to rem sts.
Bind off 4 sts, rib to end.
Work a further 29 rows, dec 1 st at beg of last row. *33 sts*
Leave these sts on a holder.

SIDE PANELS
(make 2)
One worked along left-hand side of Back, one worked along left-hand side of Front.
With RS facing, using US 6 needles and starting at cast on edge, pick up and knit 2 sts in M, then 80 sts in C. *82 sts*
Row 1: P80C, k2M.

"do you dare to make this in fluoro colors?"

Row 2: Using M, k to end.
Row 3: Using M, p to last 2 sts, k2.
Row 4: K2M, 80C.
Row 5: P80C, k2M.
Rows 6–9: Rep rows 2–3 rows twice.
Rows 10–17: Rep rows 4–5 four times.
Rows 18–21: Rep rows 2–3 twice.
Rows 22–23: Rep rows 4–5.
Rows 24–25: Rep rows 2–3.
Rows 26–27: Rep rows 4–5.
Bind off.

BUTTON BAND
With RS facing, US 6 needles and C, pick up and knit 18 sts down left side of front opening, starting 6 rows below top edge.
Row 1: P2, *k2, p2, rep from * to end.
Row 2: K2, *p2, k2, rep from * to end.
Rep the last 2 rows three more times.
Bind off in rib.

BUTTONHOLE BAND
With RS facing, US 6 needles and C, pick up and knit 18 sts up right side of front opening, ending 6 rows below top edge.
Work 3 rows rib.
Buttonhole row: Rib 2, [rib 2 tog, yo, rib 2] four times.
Work 4 more rows in rib.
Bind off.

TOP CASING
Join bound off edges of side panels to right-hand sides of Back and Front to form a tube.
With RS facing, US 6 circular needle and M, rib across sts of right side of front, pick up and knit 18 sts across row ends of side section, rib across sts of back, pick up and k 18 sts across row ends of side section, rib across sts of left side of front.
Work 4 rows in rib as set.
Bind off in rib.

FINISHING
Lap buttonhole band over button band and stitch in place at base. Fold casing to WS and stitch in place. Sew on buttons. Thread ribbon through casing.

trapeze jacket

Although this jacket is the most complicated project in the book, you'll be so proud to finish it. You might also like to know that it is part of my latest collection for winter 2007. It's heavy enough to be worn as your everyday jacket and the trapeze shape is ideal for layering. This jacket also looks amazing in bright colors and will be very useful in black.

SIZE

One size to fit sizes 6–12
Length from shoulder 21¾in
Sleeve seam 13in

YARN SUGGESTION

14 1¾oz balls of worsted-weight yarn (such as Rowan Cashsoft Aran)
1 1¾oz ball of fingering-weight yarn (such as Rowan Cashsoft 4-ply)

NEEDLES

Pair each of US 3, US 6, and US 7 knitting needles
Knitter's sewing needle

OTHER MATERIALS

G/6 crochet hook
6 buttons

GAUGE

19 stitches and 25 rows to 4in square over stockinette stitch using worsted yarn.
28 stitches and 36 rows to 4in square over stockinette stitch using fingering yarn.

ABBREVIATIONS

k2below = k into st 2 rows below next st on left needle, letting st above drop from left needle.
See also page 120.

PATTERN

LOWER BACK
Using US 7 needles and worsted-weight yarn, cast on 141 sts.
Work in textured patt as folls:
Row 1 (RS): Purl.
Row 2 and every foll alt row: Knit.
Row 3: P4, *k2below, p3, rep from * to last st, p1.
Row 5: Purl.
Row 7: P2, *k2below, p3, rep from * to last 3 sts, k2below, P2.
Row 8: As row 2.
These 8 rows form textured patt.
Cont in textured patt until back measures 12¾in, ending with a WS row.
Shape armholes
Keeping patt correct, bind off 3 sts at beg of next 2 rows. *135 sts*
Dec 1 st at each end of next 3 rows, then on foll 3 alt rows. *123 sts*
Cont straight until work measures 2½in from start of armhole shaping, ending with a WS row.
Bind off.

BACK YOKE
Using US 7 needles and worsted-weight yarn, cast on 67 sts.
Starting with a knit row, work in st st for 6¼in, ending with RS facing.
Shape shoulders and back neck

Bind off 6 sts at beg of next 2 rows. *55 sts*
Next row: Bind off 6 sts, k until there are 8 sts on right needle and turn.
Work each side of neck separately.
Bind off 3 sts at beg of next row.
Bind off rem 5 sts.
With RS facing, rejoin yarn to rem sts, bind off 27 sts, k to end.
Bind off 6 sts at beg of next row, then 3 sts at beg of foll row, ending with a RS row.
Bind off rem 5 sts.

LEFT SIDE FRONT PANEL
Using US 7 needles and worsted-weight yarn, cast on 21 sts.
Work in textured patt as for Lower Back for 12¾in, ending with a WS row.
(For Right Side Front Panel, work 1 extra row here.)
Shape armhole
Keeping patt correct, bind off 3 sts at beg of next row. *18 sts*
Work 1 row. (For Right Side Front Panel, omit this row.)
Dec 1 st at armhole edge of next 3 rows, then on foll 3 alt rows. *12 sts*
Cont straight until work measures 2½in from start of armhole shaping, ending with a WS row.
Bind off.

RIGHT SIDE FRONT PANEL

Work as for Left Side Front Panel, noting the bracketed exceptions.

LEFT CENTER FRONT PANEL

Using US 7 needles and worsted-weight yarn, cast on 50 sts.

Starting with a knit row, work in st st for 11½in, ending with a WS row.

(For Right Side Front Panel, work 1 extra row here.)

Shape pocket opening

Bind off 4 sts at beg of next row. *46 sts*

Cont straight until work measures 5in from pocket bound off edge, ending at pocket bound off edge.

Cast on 4 sts at beg of next row.

Cont straight until work measures 15¼in, ending with a WS row.

Bind off.

RIGHT CENTER FRONT PANEL

Work as for Left Side Front Panel, noting the bracketed exception.

LEFT FRONT YOKE

Using US 7 needles and worsted-weight yarn, cast on 27 sts.

Starting with a knit row, work in st st for 3½in, ending with a RS row. (For Right Front Yoke, work 1 extra row here.)

Shape neck

Bind off 3 sts at beg of next row. *24 sts*

Dec 1 st at neck edge of next 5 rows, then on foll 2 alt rows. *17 sts*

Cont straight until work measures 6¼in from cast-on edge, ending at armhole edge.

Shape shoulder

Bind off 6 sts at beg of next and foll alt row.

Work 1 row.

Bind off rem 5 sts.

RIGHT FRONT YOKE

Work as for Left Front Yoke, noting the bracketed exception.

LEFT SHOULDER PANEL

Using US 7 needles and worsted-weight yarn, cast on 25 sts.

Work in textured patt as for Lower Back for 2¾in, ending with a RS row.

(For Right Shoulder Panel, work 1 extra row here.)

Shape neck

Bind off 2 sts at beg of next row. *23 sts*

Dec 1 st at neck edge of next 5 rows, then on foll 2 alt rows. *16 sts*

Cont straight until work measures 5½in from cast-on edge, ending at armhole edge.

Shape shoulder

Bind off 5 sts at beg of next and foll alt row.

Work 1 row.

Bind off rem 6 sts.

RIGHT SHOULDER PANEL

Work as for Left Shoulder Panel, noting the bracketed exception.

SLEEVES

(both alike)

Using US 6 needles and worsted-weight yarn, cast on 43 sts.

Work in garter st for 16 rows, ending with a WS row.

Next row: Inc in first st, [k1, inc in next st] twenty-one times. *65 sts*

Change to US 7 needles.

Next row: Knit.

Work in textured patt as for Lower Back for 20 rows, ending with a WS row.

Dec 1 st at each end of next and 2 foll 10th rows. *59 sts*

Cont straight until Sleeve measures 13in, ending with a WS row.

Shape top

Bind off 3 sts at beg of next 2 rows. *53 sts*

Dec 1 st at each end of next 3 rows, then on foll 2 alt rows, then on every foll 4th row until 33 sts rem, then on foll 8 alt rows, then on foll 3 rows, ending with a WS row.

Bind off rem 11 sts.

POCKET OPENING BORDERS

(both alike)

With RS facing, using US 3 needles and fingering-weight yarn, pick up and knit 37 sts along row end edge of pocket opening edge of Center Front Panels, between bound off and cast-on edges.

Starting with a purl row, work in st st for 1½in.

Bind off.

Fold Pocket Opening Border in half to inside and slip stitch bound off edge to pick-up row on inside. Sew row end edges to bound off and cast-on edges at base and top of opening. Sew Center Front sections to Side Front sections, leaving seams open along pocket opening edge.

POCKET BAGS

(both alike)

Using US 3 needles and fingering-weight yarn, cast on 22 sts.

Starting with a knit row, work in st st, inc 1 st at each end of 2nd and foll 9 rows. *42 sts*

Work 19 rows, ending with a WS row.

Dec 1 st at beg of next and foll 4th row, then on foll 5 alt rows, then at same edge on foll 11 rows, ending with a WS row.

Bind off rem 24 sts.

Work another Pocket Bag in exactly this way, then work a further 2 Pocket Bag pieces reversing all shapings by reading k for p, RS for WS and vice versa.

Sew pairs of Pocket Bag pieces together leaving longer straight row end edge open. Now sew Pocket Bag opening to pocket opening in Center Front and Side Front panel seam.

FRONT YOKE TRIMS

(both alike)

Using US 7 needles and waste worsted-weight yarn, cast on 27 sts.

Knit 2 rows.

Join in main worsted-weight yarn.

Using main worsted-weight yarn and starting with a knit row, work in st st for 4 rows.

Break off main worsted-weight yarn.
Using waste yarn, work 1 row.
Leave sts on a spare length of yarn.
Using photograph as a guide, make
pleats across upper edge of joined
Center and Side Front sections so that
they match length of cast-on edge of
Front Yoke, then sew together. Lay
Front Yoke Trim over seam and
backstitch in place through sts of rows
where main and waste yarns meet.
Unravel waste yarn, leaving Front Yoke
Trim covering seam.

BUTTON BAND

With RS facing, using US 6 needles
and worsted-weight yarn, pick up and
knit 90 sts evenly down entire left
front opening edge, from neck shaping
of Front Yoke to cast-on edge of
Center Front.
Work in garter st for 30 rows, ending
with a RS row.
Bind off knitwise (on WS.)

BUTTONHOLE BAND

With RS facing, using US 6 needles and
worsted-weight yarn, pick up and knit
90 sts evenly up entire right front
opening edge, from cast-on edge of
Center Front to neck shaping of
Front Yoke.
Work in garter st for 13 rows, ending
with a WS row.
Row 14: K30, *bind off 2 sts (to make a
buttonhole), k until there are 16 sts on
right needle after bind off, rep from *
twice more, bind off 2 sts (to make 4th
buttonhole), k to end.
Row 15: K to end, casting on 2 sts over
those bound off on previous row.
Work in garter st for a further 15 rows,
ending with a RS row.
Bind off knitwise (on WS.)

COLLAR

Using US 6 needles and worsted-
weight yarn, cast on 123 sts.
Row 1: K1, *p1, k1, rep from * to end.
Row 2: Inc in first st, k1, *p1, k1, rep

from * to last st, inc in last st. *125 sts*
These 2 rows form rib.
Cont in rib, inc 1 st at each end of next
3 rows and taking inc sts into rib.
131 sts
Work 7 rows, ending with a WS row.
Dec 1 st at each end of next and foll
4 alt rows. *121 sts*
Work 1 row.
Bind off in rib.

COLLAR TRIM

Using US 3 needles and fingering-
weight yarn, cast on 220 sts.
Starting with a knit row, work in st st for
7 rows.
Break off main fingering-weight yarn
and join in waste fingering-weight yarn.
Work 2 rows.
Leave sts on a spare length of yarn.
Positioning cast on edge of Collar Trim
just inside edge of Collar, sew cast on
edge of Collar Trim to cast on and
shaped row end edges of Collar, easing
Trim around curved edges and leaving
Collar bound off edge free. Fold Trim in
half so that it encloses outer edge of
Collar and back stitch in place through
sts of last row of main yarn. Unravel
waste yarn, leaving Trim covering edge.

FINISHING

Using photograph as a guide, make
pleats across upper edge of Lower
Back so that this edge fits cast on
edge of Back Yoke and sew pieces
together. Lay Shoulder Panels onto
Front Yokes so that armhole, neck and
shoulder edges match, and sew
together along these edges. Join
shoulder, side and sleeve seams. Sew
sleeves into armholes. Sew bound off
edge of Collar to neck edge,
positioning folded ends of Collar Trim
half way across top of Front Bands.
Sew buttons onto Button Band to
correspond with buttonholes, then sew
rem 2 buttons through Shoulder Panel
and Front Yokes as in photograph.
Using G/6 crochet hook, attach
worsted-weight yarn at base of Button
Band pick-up row and work 1 row of
double crochet around entire lower
edge, ending at base of Buttonhole
Band pick-up row. Fasten off.
Work 1 row of double crochet along
top edges of Front Bands to start
of collar.

cap-sleeve cardigan

This easy cardigan shape is great for first-time clothes knitters as there's just a hint of shaping. The lace-effect yoke means that wearing a top in a contrast color will make the knit even more effective and show it off to best advantage: everyone will know how clever and talented you are. If you have a top that you plan to wear underneath, you could match the buttons to your top as I've done, which will accentuate the contrast. For a summer cover-up this little cardi will work beautifully in cotton.

SIZE

Actual measurements
Bust 35½in
Length to shoulder 21¼in

YARN SUGGESTION

6 1¾oz balls of sport-weight yarn
(such as Rowan Pure Wool DK)

NEEDLES

Pair each of US 5 and US 6
knitting needles
Knitter's sewing needle

OTHER MATERIALS

Three buttons

GAUGE

22 stitches and 30 rows to 4in
square over stockinette stitch
using US 6 needles.

ABBREVIATIONS

See page 120.

PATTERN

BACK

With US 5 needles, cast on 117 sts.
Row 1: K1, *p1, k1, rep from * to end.
Row 2: P1, *k1, p1, rep from * to end.
Rep the last 2 rows twice more.
Change to US 6 needles.
Beg with a knit row, cont in st st.
Work 8 rows.
Dec row: K8, skpo, k to last 10 sts, k2 tog, k8.
Work 9 rows st st.
Rep the last 10 rows eight more times.
Work the dec row once more. *97 sts*
Cont straight until back measures 14½in from cast on edge, ending with a purl row.
Cont in lace patt as folls:
Row 1: K1, *yo, k2, sl 1, k2 tog, psso, k2, yo, k1, rep from * to end.
Row 2: P to end.
Row 3: K2, *yo, k1, sl 1, k2 tog, psso, k1, yo, k3, rep from * to last 7 sts, yo, k1, sl 1, k2 tog, psso, k1, yo, k2.
Row 4: P to end.
Row 5: K3, *yo, sl 1, k2 tog, psso, yo, k5, rep from * to last 6 sts, yo, sl 1, k2 tog, psso, yo, k3.
Row 6: P to end.
These 6 rows form the lace patt and are repeated
Work straight until back measures 21¼in from cast on edge, ending with a wrong side row.
Shape shoulders
Bind off 8 sts at beg of next 6 rows and 7 sts at beg of foll 2 rows. *35 sts*
Change to US 5 needles.
Row 1: K1, *p1, k1, rep from * to end.
Row 2: P1, *k1, p1, rep from * to end.
Rep the last 2 rows twice more.
Bind off in rib.

LEFT FRONT

With US 5 needles, cast on 59 sts.
Row 1: P1, *k1, p1, rep from * to end.
Row 2: K1, *p1, k1, rep from * to end.
Rep the last 2 rows twice more.
Change to US 6 needles.
Beg with a knit row, cont in st st.
Work 8 rows.
Dec row: K8, skpo, k to end.
Work 9 rows st st.
Rep the last 10 rows eight more times.
Rep the dec row once more. *49 sts*

" for summer, this
cute cardi will
work beautifully
in cotton "

Cont straight until front measures 14½in from cast on edge, ending with a purl row.

Cont in lace patt as folls:

Row 1: K1, *yo, k2, sl 1, k2 tog, psso, k2, yo, k1, rep from * to end.

Row 2: P to end.

Row 3: K2, *yo, k1, sl 1, k2 tog, psso, k1, yo, k3, rep from * to last 7 sts, yo, k1, sl 1, k2 tog, psso, k1, yo, k2.

Row 4: P to end.

Row 5: K3, *yo, sl 1, k2 tog, psso, yo, k5, rep from * to last 6 sts, yo, sl 1, k2 tog, psso, yo, k3.

Row 6: P to end.

These 6 rows form the patt and are repeated.

Neck shaping

Next row: Patt to last 3 sts, k2 tog, k1.

Next row: P to end.

Rep the last 2 rows until 31 sts rem.

Work straight until front measures same as Back to shoulder, ending at armhole edge.

Shape shoulder

Bind off 8 sts at beg of next and 2 foll alt rows.

Work 1 row.

Bind off rem 7 sts.

RIGHT FRONT

With US 5 needles cast on 59 sts.

Row 1: P1, *k1, p1, rep from * to end.

Row 2: K1, *p1, k1, rep from * to end.

Rep the last 2 rows twice more.

Change to US 6 needles.

Beg with a knit row, cont in st st.

Work 8 rows.

Dec row: K to last 10 sts, k2 tog, k8.

Work 9 rows st st.

Rep the last 10 rows eight more times.

Rep the dec row once more. *49 sts*

Cont straight until front measures 14½in from cast on edge, ending with a purl row.

Cont in lace patt as folls:

Row 1: K1, *yo, k2, sl 1, k2 tog, psso, k2, yo, k1, rep from * to end.

Row 2: P to end.

Row 3: K2, *yo, k1, sl 1, k2 tog, psso, k1, yo, k3, rep from * to last 7 sts, yo, k1, sl 1, k2 tog, psso, k1, yo, k2.

Row 4: P to end.

Row 5: K3, *yo, sl 1, k2 tog, psso, yo, k5, rep from * to last 6 sts, yo, sl 1, k2 tog, psso, yo, k3.

Row 6: P to end.

These 6 rows form the patt and are repeated.

Neck shaping

Next row: K1, skpo, patt to end.

Next row: P to end.

Rep the last 2 rows until 31 sts rem.

Work straight until front measures same as Back to shoulder, ending at armhole edge.

Shape shoulder

Bind off 8 sts at beg of next and 2 foll alt rows.

Work 1 row.

Bind off rem 7 sts.

BUTTON BAND

With RS facing and US 5 needles, pick up and knit 47 sts to beg of neck shaping, then 86 sts to cast on edge. *133 sts*

Row 1: K1, *p1, k1, rep from * to end.

Row 2: P1, *k1, p1, rep from * to end.

Rep the last 2 rows once more and the 1st row again.

Bind off in rib.

BUTTONHOLE BAND

With RS facing and US 5 needles, pick up and knit 86 sts to beg of neck shaping, then 47 sts to shoulder. *133 sts*

Row 1: K1, *p1, k1, rep from * to end.

Row 2: P1, *k1, p1, rep from * to end.

Buttonhole row: Rib 52, [rib 2 tog, yo twice, rib 2 tog, rib 8] twice, rib 2 tog, yo twice, rib 2 tog, rib to end.

Work 2 more rows in rib.

Bind off.

ARMBANDS

(both alike)

Join shoulder seams.

With right side facing, using US 5 needles and starting and ending at first row of lace patt, pick up and knit 96 sts evenly.

Work 5 rows in rib.

Bind off in rib.

FINISHING

Join side and armband seams. Sew on buttons.

embellishing your knitting

Now that you've done all the knitting, this is where you can really get creative and have some fun. It doesn't take much to turn a plain knitted project into something that all your friends will envy, especially when you tell them that you did it all yourself.

On the following pages you will find ideas for materials to use as embellishments, examples of knitwear that have been transformed with the help of a few sequins, a bow, or some buttons, plus some useful techniques for making cords and pom-poms, embroidering, and sewing on sequins.

embellishments

All kinds of trimmings, buttons, and motifs can be used to add glamour and cute style to knitwear. Here are examples of materials to look for, so keep an eye out in craft and vintage stores, on the Internet, and don't forget to raid your grandma's button box.

buttons

Become a button hoarder and as your collection grows you will always have just what you need for a project. Look out for vintage bargains, colorful contemporary buttons, and don't hesitate to re-cycle buttons from old clothes. Buttons are not just a decorative and practical solution for fastening items, they can also be used purely as embellishments (see the button-trimmed beret, page 92.)

trimmings and motifs

There is a huge variety of trimmings available that will look fabulous on your knitwear. Notions stores are a good source, but also keep an eye out for vintage pieces that are in good condition. Choose sparkling sequin motifs to add glitz, or sumptuous trim for a luxurious look.

attaching embellishments

It's always best to sew on your trimmings once the knitting itself is finished and sewn up. That way you can best judge what the finished effect will be before actually sewing on the decorations. I always sew embellishments on by hand as it is usually neatest this way, and it really doesn't take long. Choose a sewing thread to match the embellishment rather than the knitting and use an ordinary sewing needle. Don't pull the stitches too tight or you will gather up the knitted fabric and spoil the shape of the garment. If the piece has to be stretched to get it on—for example, the neck of a sweater—then be aware that sewing on a trimming can stop the knitting being elastic enough. See pages 94–97 for some embellishment techniques.

ribbons

Maybe the most versatile trim of all, ribbons come in such a wide range of colors and fabrics that you are bound to find something to suit your own project. I love bows, so ribbons are a favorite item and find a home on all sorts of pieces (see Bow Beanie, page 52.)

lace

Available both as a trimming and as motif pieces, lace can give a sweet girly touch to a knitted item. Use it as a trim (see Lacy Long Gloves, page 18), or appliqué pieces onto a plain hat (see Embellished Beret, page 60.)

embellishment ideas

Here are some ideas for decorating your knitted projects, but I urge you to let your creativity blossom and develop your own style.

A plain hat with earflaps can be embroidered with snowflakes and sequins for a winter wonderland look. The snowflakes are made from simple straight stitches worked in sport-weight yarn.

A border of narrow lace emphasizes the delicate look of lace knitwear. Here, it has been stitched to the top of lacy legwarmers and a ribbon runs just below it for an extra finishing touch.

A selection of vintage buttons, individually stitched on, make a quick, simple, and yet stylish addition to your plain beret.

Sequins look fabulous on knitting and can be sewn on in any shape you wish. Use them to highlight details such as shaping, or just to add sparkle. See page 94 for the best method of sewing them on.

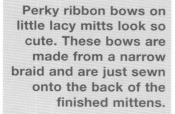

Perky ribbon bows on little lacy mitts look so cute. These bows are made from a narrow braid and are just sewn onto the back of the finished mittens.

A big, flat bow adds a 1920s look to a very modern knitted beanie. It's amazing how much difference even a small embellishment can make.

buttonholes

Overcasting the edges of buttonholes both reinforces them and decorates them. Use a contrast color yarn to add an extra finishing touch. If the yarn is very thick it may be best to split it into two, as chunky yarn can look a bit lumpy embroidered in this way.

1 Thread a knitter's sewing needle with a long length of yarn. From the back, bring the needle up one stitch out from the edge of the buttonhole. Take the needle through the buttonhole and up through the knitting again, always keeping one stitch out from the edge for the neatest finish.

2 When you have worked right around the buttonhole, turn the knitting over. On the back, thread the tails from the beginning and end of the embroidery through the backs of the stitches to secure them.

Above Worked neatly these buttonholes look really effective.

sequins

Sequins add lovely sparkle to items such as the Sequined Earmuffs (see page 56.) Here the technique is shown on garter stitch fabric, but you work it in exactly the same way on stockinette stitch.

1 Thread a sewing needle with sewing thread. Lay the sequin in position and, from the back, bring the needle through the hole in the middle of the sequin. Take it back down close to the edge.

2 Bring the needle back up through the middle, then back down close to the opposite edge.

Above It might sound time-consuming to sew on sequins by hand, but it's actually quicker than you might think, and the effect is well worth the effort.

swiss darning

Also known as "duplicate stitch" this is a way of adding different-colored stitches to a piece of knitting once it is finished. Always work Swiss darning using a yarn that is the same weight as the yarn the fabric is knitted in or it won't look very neat. Use this technique to embroider the Bow Beanie (see page 52),and Short and Long Fleur-de-Lys Gloves (see page 10.)

a vertical row Use this method to work vertical rows of colored stitches.

1 Thread a knitter's sewing needle with a long length of yarn. From the back, bring the needle up through the knitted fabric at the base of a stitch. *Take the needle under the two loops of the stitch above, as shown.

2 Gently pull the yarn through, then take the needle back down through the base of the stitch, where it came out.

3 Bring the yarn up through the knitted fabric at the base of the next stitch up. Repeat from * until the row is stitched.

a horizontal row Use this method to work horizontal rows of colored stitches.

1 From the back, bring the needle up through the knitted fabric at the base of a stitch. Take the needle under the two loops of the stitch above and back down where it came out, as before. Bring the needle up through the base of the next stitch to the left to work the horizontal row.

Above Work your Swiss darning neatly and it will look just like the rest of the knitting.

making cord

Twisted cord can be used to hang pom-poms from (see Hat with Cable Earflaps, page 62), lace up buttonholes and thread through eyelets instead of ribbon, and you can make it to exactly match your knitting. Ask a friend to help you; it makes the job easier.

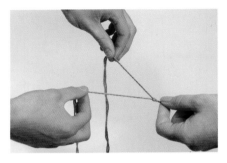

1 Cut lengths of yarn approximately 30 percent longer than you want the finished cord to be. Knot them together at one end and ask your friend to hold the knot. Divide the lengths into two groups and, holding one group in each hand, twist them in the same direction. Move your hands down the yarn as you twist so that you twist the entire length.

2 When the lengths are so twisted that they are beginning to kink up, bring the ends together. Holding the ends tightly, tell your friend to let go of the knot. The yarn will coil up, twisting around itself. Knot the ends you are holding and pull gently on both ends to smooth out the kinks and create a twisted cord.

Above Make the cord as thin or thick as you want, and in as many colors as you want, by simply using more strands of yarn.

french knitting

This used to be worked on a wooden cotton reel with nails hammered into the top of it. You can buy French knitting kits now, which work in just the same way.

Your kit will come with instructions, so read them carefully. Basically, you are just winding the yarn around each pin in turn in the top of the bobbin and lifting the first loop over the second one. The knitted cord grows quite quickly, particularly if you are using chunky yarn.

Left Make cord to match or contrast with your knitting and use it for handles (see Gold Clutch Bag, page 36), and joining mittens (see Cabled Mittens, page 16.)

making pom-poms

Fun to make and cute as an embellishment, pom-poms are just great. You can buy plastic circles to wind them on, but card cut from a breakfast cereal box works just as well.

1 Cut two identical circles of card with smaller circles cut out of the middle. The larger the outer circle, the bigger the pom-pom and the larger the inner circle, the denser the pom-pom will be.

2 Lay the circles one on top of the other and start to wind yarn around and through them, as shown.

3 Keep winding, cutting lengths of yarn and using those as the hole gets too small for the ball to pass through.

4 When the hole in the middle is filled with yarn, use sharp embroidery scissors to carefully cut through the wound yarn around the outer edges of the circle.

5 Separate the card circles just a little. Cut another length of yarn and slip it between them. Pulling the yarn as tight as possible, tie it in a very firm double knot. Wrap the yarn around to the other side and knot it again to hold the pom-pom securely together.

6 Carefully cut away the card circles. Use the embroidery threads to trim any protruding ends of yarn.

Left Make a single-color pom-pom, as here, or by winding on layers of different colored yarns you can make stripy ones.

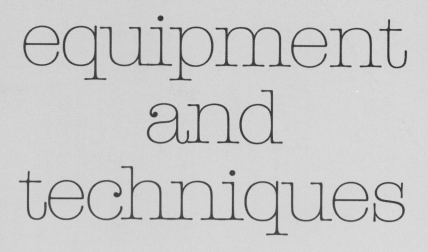

equipment and techniques

There are only four simple techniques to master and then you too are a knitter: cast on, knit, purl and bind off. Every single other thing you will ever need to do to knit a pattern is a variation on one or another of these techniques.

To start knitting you only need a pair of needles and some yarn, but there are a few other things that will be helpful. On the following pages you will find all you need to have and know to knit the projects in this book. For information on the different yarns used and how to swap them with other yarns you may want to use, turn to page 118.

knitting equipment

As well as some yarn and needles, you will need some of this knitting paraphernalia to make some of the projects in this book.

1 Knitting needles come in various sizes and materials; left to right, bamboo, metal, and plastic. Each knitting pattern gives the size of needle you need, but the material is up to you. Novice knitters may find bamboo needles easiest to use as the yarn does not slip so easily on them, making dropping a stitch less likely.

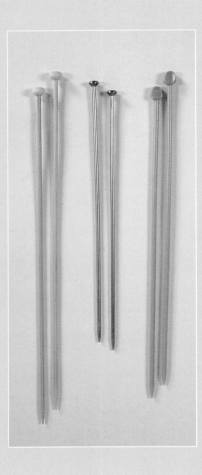

2 Double-pointed needles have, as the name suggests, a point at each end. They are used for knitting projects in the round—projects with out a seam, such as the Simple Snood on page 44.

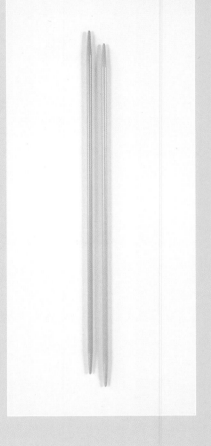

3 Use a cable needle when working projects such as the Hat with Cable Earflaps on page 62. The needle shown is a cranked one, which holds the stitches securely while you work the cable, but you can also buy straight cable needles, which are quicker to use.

4 Stitch holders are used to keep some stitches safe while you work on another part of the project. They usually look like giant safety pins (top), but the double-ended type (below) are useful as you can knit straight off them rather than having to put the stitches back on a knitting needle first.

5 Knitter's pins (right) have blunt points to help prevent them splitting the yarn when you pin projects together before sewing up.

6 Like knitter's pins, knitter's sewing needles (far right) have a blunt point to help prevent them splitting the yarn when you are sewing up a project.

7 Use a solid ruler, either metal or plastic, to measure your tension (see page 116.)

8 Keep a pair of small, sharp scissors to hand for cutting yarn. Don't try and break yarn with your hands, some types are surprisingly strong.

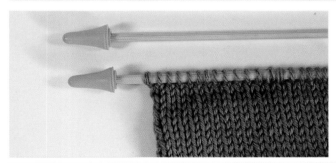

9 Point protectors are not essential, but they are useful. They stop the stitches falling off your needle when you are not knitting, and they stop the points of your needles punching holes in your knitting bag.

10 A row counter is another non-essential item that you might find useful. Put it on a knitting needle and clock up each row as you work it, then you will never loose your place in a pattern.

knitting techniques

Mastering and practising the following techniques will enable you to knit any of the projects in this book.

holding yarn and needles

There is no right or wrong way of holding the yarn and needles, so try these two most popular methods and use whichever feels most comfortable.

In the USA and UK the usual way is to hold the left-hand needle from above, rather like a knife, and the right-hand needle in the crook of your thumb, rather like a pen. The working end of the yarn goes over the right index finger, under the second finger, and over the ring finger to help control the gauge of the stitches. The right index finger moves back and forth to wind the yarn around the tip of the right-hand needle.

The other method, often called the "continental method", also holds the right-hand needle like a pen, but the left-hand needle is held between the thumb and second finger. The working yarn goes over the left index finger, under the second and ring fingers, and over the little finger to control the gauge. The left index finger is held aloft and moves back and forth to wind the yarn around the tip of the right-hand needle.

slip knot

The starting point for any piece of knitting is a slip knot. There is more than one way of making this, but the result is the same.

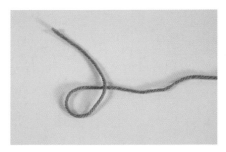

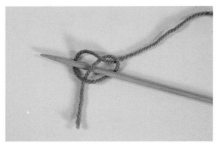

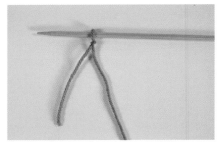

1 Lay the tail end of the yarn over the ball end to form a loop.

2 Bring the tail end under the loop of yarn. Slip the tip of a knitting needle under this tail end, as shown.

3 Pull on both ends of the yarn and the slip knot will tighten around the needle. This will always be your first cast on stitch. After you have knitted the first couple of rows, you can pull gently on the tail end of the yarn to tighten the first stitch if necessary.

thumb cast on

This cast on has an elastic edge that matches in well with the look of garter, rib, and seed stitch (see page 110.) If you are working in double-knitting yarn, making a slip knot about 1 yard from the end will allow you to cast on about 80 stitches.

1 Make a slip knot about the necessary distance from the end of the yarn. Hold the needle with the knot on in your right hand. *Wind the tail end of the yarn clockwise around your left thumb.

2 Put the tip of the needle under the loop of yarn around your thumb.

3 With your right index finger, wind the ball end of the yarn around the tip of the needle, taking it between the needle and your thumb and then around to the front.

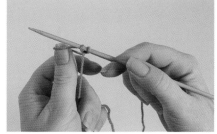

4 Bring the knitting needle, and the ball end loop around it, through the loop on your thumb, slipping the loop off your thumb as you do so. Pull gently on the tail end of the yarn to tighten the stitch.

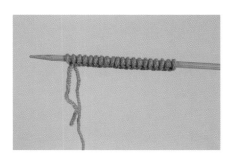

5 Repeat from * until you have cast the number of stitches needed onto the needle.

cable cast on

This method of casting on produces a neat, firm edge that matches in perfectly with the look of stockinette stitch. Always make the slip knot about 6in from the end of the yarn to leave enough to weave in the end later.

1 Hold the needle with the knot on in your left hand. From left to right, put the tip of the right-hand needle into the front of the knot. *Wind the ball end of the yarn around the tip of the right-hand needle, going under and then over the top of the needle.

2 Bring the right-hand knitting needle, and the loop of yarn around the tip of it, through the slip knot.

3 Slip the loop of yarn on the right-hand needle onto the left-hand needle and pull gently on the ball end of the yarn to tighten the stitch. You have cast on a second stitch.

4 For all the following stitches, put the right-hand needle between the two previous stitches, instead of through the last stitch.

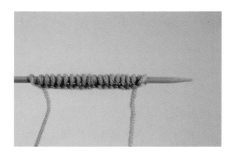

5 Repeat from * until you have cast the number of stitches needed onto the needle.

knit stitch

This is the first and most basic stitch you need to learn to start knitting, and it is very similar to the cable cast on (see opposite.) First cast on the number of stitches needed for the project, using whichever cast on method you prefer.

1 Hold the needle with the cast on stitches in your left hand. *From left to right, put the tip of the right-hand needle into the front of the first stitch.

2 Wind the working yarn around the tip of the right-hand needle, going under and then over the top of the needle.

3 Bring the right-hand needle, and the loop of yarn around it, through the stitch on the left-hand needle.

4 Keeping the loop on the right-hand needle, slip the first stitch off the left-hand needle. You have knitted one stitch. Repeat from * until you have knitted all the stitches on the left-hand needle. Then swap the needles in your hands and you are ready to begin the next row.

purl stitch

This is the other basic stitch used in knitting. It is really just a variation on knit stitch and is no more difficult to learn.

1 Hold the needle with the stitches in your left hand. *From right to left, put the tip of the right-hand needle into the front of the first stitch.

2 From front to back, wind the working yarn over the tip of the right-hand needle.

3 Bring the right-hand needle, and the loop of yarn around it, through the stitch on the left-hand needle.

4 Keeping the loop on the right-hand needle, slip the first stitch off the left-hand needle. You have purled one stitch. Repeat from * until you have purled all the stitches on the left-hand needle. Then swap the needles in your hands and you are ready to begin the next row.

binding off

This is the way you finish off your knitting, securing the stitches so that they don't unravel. It is shown here on a knit row, but can be worked just as well on a purl row: simply purl the stitches instead of knitting them.

1 Knit the first two stitches on the left-hand needle.

2 *Put the tip of the left-hand needle into the first stitch you knitted and lift it over the second stitch. Drop this first stitch off both needles.

3 Knit another stitch and repeat from * to bind off all the stitches in turn.

4 When you have just one stitch left on the right-hand needle, pull gently to open it up a little and slip it off the needle. Cut the yarn 6in from the knitting. Thread the cut end through the last stitch and pull gently on the cut end to tighten the stitch.

increases

Increasing is making extra stitches in a row to make the knitting wider. There are various ways of doing this, but shown here are the two most commonly used methods.

increase (inc) This method involves knitting twice into a stitch. The increase is visible in the finished knitting as the second stitch made has a small bar of yarn across the bottom of it.

1 Knit to the position of the increase. Knit into the next stitch in the usual way (see page 105), but do not drop the original stitch off the left-hand needle.

2 Now knit into the back of the same stitch on the left-hand needle, then drop it off the needle.
You have made two stitches out of one and so increased by one stitch.

make one (M1) This method involves creating a brand new stitch between two existing ones. It is almost completely invisible in the finished knitting.

1 Knit to the position of the increase. Using the tip of the left-hand needle, pick up the loop of yarn lying between the next two stitches. Pick it up by putting the tip of the needle through the front of the loop.

2 Knit into the back of the picked-up loop on the left-hand needle, then drop the loop.
You have created a completely new stitch and so increased by one stitch.

decreases

Decreasing involves taking away stitches in a row to make the knitting narrower. Again, there are different ways of doing this, but shown here are the two most popular methods. These decreases slant in different directions, so when used at either end of a row, they mirror each other.

knit two together (k2tog) In this method you knit two stitches together to make one. The decrease slants to the right on a knit row.

1 Knit to the position of the decrease. From left to right, put the tip of the right-hand needle through the front of the second stitch from the end of the left-hand needle, then through the first one. Knit the two stitches together in the usual way, just as if they were one.
You have made two stitches into one and so decreased by one stitch.

slip one, knit one pass slipped stitch over (skpo) This method involves slipping a stitch and then passing the next one over it, rather like binding off. This decrease slants to the left on a knit row.

1 Knit to the position of the decrease. Insert the right-hand needle into the next stitch, as if you were going to knit it, but slip it from the left-hand to the right-hand needle without knitting it.

2 Knit the next stitch on the left-hand needle in the usual way.

3 Put the tip of the left-hand needle into the slipped stitch and lift it over the knitted stitch, then drop it off both needles.
You have made two stitches into one and so decreased by one stitch.

knitted fabrics

Now that you can knit, you can create knitted fabrics with different stitch patterns. Shown here are swatches of the four most popular simple knitted fabrics.

garter stitch This is the most basic knitted fabric as it is made with knit stitches only.

To work garter stitch, cast on as many stitches as you need.
Knit every row. That's all there is to it.

stockinette stitch (st st) This is the most popular knitted fabric and made by working alternate rows of knit and purl stitches. The other side of this fabric is called reverse stockinette stitch (rev st st.)

To work stockinette stitch, cast on as many stitches as you need.
Row 1: Knit.
Row 2: Purl.
Repeat rows 1–2. It's not really any more difficult than garter stitch.
If you get confused as to whether you should be knitting or purling on the next row, just hold the needle with the stitches on in your left hand and look at the side facing you. If that is the right side, as shown above, then the next row will be a knit row. If the wrong side is facing you, the next row will be a purl row.

rib stitch This is usually used to make cuffs and collars as it is very stretchy. There are various types of rib stitch, shown here is single rib (1x1 rib.) Variations on this are worked by knitting and purling different numbers of stitches: for example, to work double rib (2x2 rib), you knit two stitches, then purl two.

To work single rib stitch, cast on an odd number of stitches.
Row 1: [K1, p1] rep to last st, k1.
Row 2: [P1, k1] rep to last st, p1.
Repeat rows 1–2.
After you have knitted the first stitch, bring the yarn between the tips of the needles to the front of the work ready to purl the next stitch. When you have purled, take the yarn to the back again to knit the next stitch.

seed stitch This is a decorative stitch that makes a flat, firm border on garments and accessories.

To work seed stitch, cast on an odd number of stitches.
Row 1: [K1, p1] rep to last st, k1.
Repeat row 1.
Bring the yarn forward to purl and take it back again to knit in the same way as for rib stitch. If you get confused as to which stitch you should be working next, look at the previous one. If it has a bump across it then it is a purl stitch and the next stitch will be knit. If the last stitch is smooth, then you knitted it and the next stitch will be purl.

cables

Cabling is one of those techniques that looks difficult, but is in fact easy. All you are doing is swapping the positions on the needle of groups of stitches. Shown here is cable six, but you can cable two, four, or eight stitches just as easily. Cables are usually worked in stockinette stitch with a background of reverse stockinette stitch, as shown here.

cable six front (C6F) A front (or "forward", as it is also known), cable twists to the left.

1 Purl to the position of the cable. Take the yarn between the tips of the needles to the back of the work. Slip the next three stitches on the left-hand needle onto a cable needle and leave this at the front of the work.

2 Knit the next three stitches on the left-hand needle. Just ignore the cable needle while doing this.

3 Now knit the three stitches on the cable needle. Just slide them to the end of the needle and knit them in the usual way. Purl to the end of the row, or to the next cable.

cable six back (C6B) A back cable twists to the right.

1 Work a back cable in a similar way to a front cable. The only difference is that once you have slipped the three stitches onto the cable needle, you leave it at the back of the work instead of at the front.

Above This swatch of C6F is worked over eight rows; that is to say, the cable is twisted on every eighth row of the knitting.

color knitting

There are two main techniques for color knitting, but in this book only the Fair Isle technique is used. It is important to twist the yarns around one another as shown to prevent holes appearing between the different-colored yarns.

1 On a knit row, knit to the first stitch to be worked in a different color. Bring the new color yarn under the original color yarn and then around the needle to knit the stitch. Here a blue stitch will become a cream one.

2 Knit the stitches in the new color. When you get to the first stitch to be knitted in the original color, bring that yarn under the new color and around the needle to knit the stitch. Here a cream stitch will become a blue one.

3 On a purl row, purl to the first stitch to be worked in a different color. Bring the new color yarn under the original color and then around the needle to purl the stitch. Here a cream stitch will become a blue one.

4 Bring the working yarn (here it is cream), over the original yarn (blue), and purl the stitches. When you reach the first stitch to be worked in a different color, bring the new color yarn under the original color and then around the needle to purl the stitch. Here a blue stitch will become a cream one.

5 if you are working more than three stitches in a new color, you need to weave the original color yarn into the back of the work to prevent long strands appearing on the back. On both knit and purl rows the technique is the same; here it is shown on a purl row. Simply bring the working yarn (here it is cream), under the original yarn (blue), before taking the working yarn around the needle to purl or knit the next stitch.

Above When the yarns are twisted each time the color changes, there will be no holes between the colored sections.

lace knitting

This is often thought to be difficult, and very complex patterns can indeed be tricky. However, the lace patterns in this book are simple; just follow the pattern, keeping count of your stitches across the row and all will be well.

eyelets These are the staple ingredient of lace knitting. An eyelet is a small hole that when arranged with others in a pattern produces the lace effect. Eyelets worked in this way are also used to make buttonholes for small buttons.

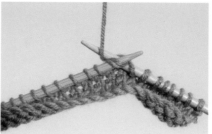

1 On a knit row, knit to the position of the eyelet. Bring the yarn forward between the tips of the knitting needles (yarnover, yo.)

2 Take the yarn over the top of the right-hand needle and to the back, ready to knit the next two stitches on the left-hand needle together (k2tog.)

3 When you are purling back across the stitches, purl the yarnover as if it were a normal stitch.

Left A pattern of eyelets offset by one stitch on each knit row produces a simple yet effective knitted lace.

slipped stitches Another technique often used in lace knitting, slipped stitches can be worked knitwise or purlwise. If the pattern does not specify which way to slip a stitch, slip it knitwise on a knit row and purlwise on a purl row.

1 Slip a stitch knitwise by putting the right-hand needle into the next stitch, as if to knit it, but slip it onto the needle without actually knitting it. Bring the yarn across behind the slipped stitch to work the next stitch.

2 Slip a stitch purlwise by putting the right-hand needle into the next stitch, as if to purl it, but slip it onto the needle without actually purling it. Bring the yarn across behind the slipped stitch to work the next stitch.

joining in new yarn

When you reach the end of a ball of yarn you need to join in a new one in order to continue knitting your project. You will also use this method to join in a different-colored yarn when you are using the Fair Isle technique (see page 112.)

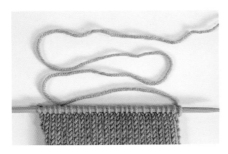

1 It is best to join in a new ball at the end of a row. To see if you have enough yarn to knit one more row, lay it out as shown. You must have a length of yarn approximately four times the width of the knitting to knit a single row.

2 Tie the new yarn in a loose single knot around the tail end of the old yarn. Slide the knot up to the work and pull it tight. Leave at least a 6in tail on each piece of yarn to be woven in later.

weaving in ends

When you have finished your knitting, you need to weave in any ends from casting on, binding off and joining in new yarn.

1 Thread a knitter's sewing needle with the tail of yarn. Take the needle back and forth, not up and over, through the backs of several stitches. Go through approximately four stitches in one direction, then work back through the last two again. If you are weaving in ends from Fair Isle knitting, weave the tails into stitches of the same color to stop them showing on the front.

blocking

Once you have finished your knitting project, it will benefit from being blocked. This smooths out the fabric, helps hide any small imperfections and makes the project much easier to sew up.

1 On an ironing board, lay out your project pieces without stretching them. Measure each piece and ease them to the correct size and shape. Pin the pieces to the board by pushing dressmaker's pins through the edge stitches into the board.

Carefully following the instructions on the yarn ball band, press all the pieces. Leave them pinned out until they are completely cold. Then take out all the pins and you are ready to start sewing up your project.

sewing up

Many people rush this stage of making a knitting project, which is a mistake. Take your time and your seams will be smooth and neat, giving your knitting a professional finish.

1 Thread a knitter's sewing needle with a long length of the yarn you used to knit the project in. (If the yarn is very fine or breaks easily, use a stronger one in the same fiber and color.) Here, a contrast color yarn has been used so that you can clearly see what is happening. Secure the yarn on the back of one of the pieces to be joined by taking it over a couple of stitches, a couple of times.

2 Bring the needle to the front of the fabric, bringing it up between the first two stitches on the first row.

3 Right-side up, lay the other project piece to be joined next to the first piece. From the front, take the needle through the fabric between the first two stitches on the first row and up under the bars of two stitches.

4 Pull the yarn through. Take the needle back through where it came out on the first project piece and up under the bars of two stitches. Pull the yarn through. Take the needle back to the other piece, through where it came out and up under the bars of two stitches. Continue in this way, zigzagging between the two pieces and taking the needle under two stitch bars each time. Gently pull on the yarn to close the seam as you work.

Above Worked neatly, a mattress stitched seam blends in to knitted fabrics well.

gauge

When you buy a pattern it will specify the yarn you should use to knit it and the gauge the pattern requires. This is the number of stitches and rows to a specific measurement, usually 4in. It is important that you work to the gauge the pattern asks for or the finished garment will be too big (if your gauge is too loose), or too small (if your gauge is too tight.)

For this reason you must always knit a gauge swatch, even if you have knitted another pattern in the specified yarn, as gauges do vary from pattern to pattern depending on the knitwear designer.

When knitting accessories that don't need a specific fit, such as the Gold Clutch Bag on page 36, or the Beehive Scarf on page 42, it is not vital that you achieve an exact gauge. However, it is still worth knitting a swatch as if your gauge is too loose, you might find that the stitch pattern doesn't look right. Also, you might run out of yarn if your gauge is loose and you are therefore using more yarn than the designer did to make each stitch.

So, even though you are desperate to start your project, take an hour or so to knit a swatch and measure it carefully. In the long run this takes much less time (and prevents a lot of disappointment), than knitting the whole project and finding that it doesn't fit.

Accessories often don't require exact gauge as it doesn't matter if they are a little bigger or smaller than stated.

knitting a gauge swatch

First, find the gauge information in the pattern. It will say something like: "22 stitches and 28 rows to 4in square over stockinette stitch using US 6 needles". What this means is that, using the right sort of yarn and needles and working the right stitch pattern, in a piece of knitting measuring 4in by 4in you must have 22 stitches in one direction and 28 rows in the other direction.

So, use the yarn and needles specified in the pattern to cast on the number of stitches stated, plus ten. Knit the number of rows stated—in the stitch pattern specified—plus ten, then bind off. Make the bind off as loose as you can to avoid pulling in the top edge of the knitting.

measuring your gauge

The next step is to measure your gauge. Do this carefully, or knitting the swatch will have been a waste of your time. It is important to measure a few stitches or rows in from the edges as the cast on and bound off edges and the row ends can be tighter or looser than the stitches in the middle of the knitting, which are the ones that matter here.

Lay the swatch flat, without stretching it at all. To count the number of stitches, lay a ruler across the swatch so that 4in (or the distance stated in the pattern), is measured out a few stitches in from either edge. Put a knitter's pin into the swatch either end of the measured distance. Remove the ruler and count the number of stitches between the pins. To count the number of rows, repeat the process, but lay the ruler vertically on the swatch so that 4in is measured out a few rows from either edge.

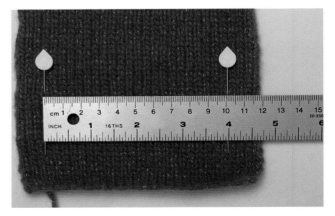

Measuring stitches on a gauge swatch.

altering your gauge

If you have the same numbers of stitches and rows as stated in the pattern, then you have the correct gauge. You can go ahead and knit the project your fingers have been itching for.

However, if you do not have the right numbers of stitches and rows, you need to alter your gauge. Do not do this by trying to knit more tightly or loosely. Everyone has a "natural" gauge, the gauge they automatically knit to, and if you try to knit to a different gauge your stitches will just be uneven. Also, you will usually forget at some point that you are trying to knit more tightly and your natural gauge will reassert itself, then you are back to square one.

The way to alter your gauge is to change the size of the knitting needles you are using. If you have too few stitches and rows, knit the swatch again using needles one size smaller. So, if the pattern asks for US 8 needles, try again using US 7 needles.

If you have too many stitches and rows, then try again with needles one size larger: US 9 needles instead of US 8.

This may sound time-consuming and annoying, but, as I said before, it's much better to knit a little square a few times than to spend more time and effort knitting a whole project that doesn't fit.

When a project uses a particular stitch pattern, you will usually be asked to work the gauge swatch in the same pattern. Don't cheat and work the swatch in stockinette stitch as it will be useless in establishing whether your gauge is correct. Knitting the swatch also gives you an opportunity to practise the stitch pattern.

yarn information

Rather than specifying an exact yarn, each project in this book gives you a yarn suggestion, which tells you the weight of yarn you should use to knit it. In brackets following this is the brand name of a yarn of the right weight. We hope that this more flexible approach will encourage you to choose your own yarns with which to knit the projects, thereby personalising them even more. Here is information on the yarns specified in this book.

Rowan Big Wool
100% wool; 87yd/3½oz ball.

Rowan Little Big Wool
67% wool, 33% nylon; 65yd/1¾oz ball.

Rowan Cashsoft Chunky
57% extra-fine merino wool, 33% acrylic microfiber, 10% cashmere; 55yd/1¾oz ball.

Rowan Cashsoft 4-ply
57% extra-fine merino wool, 33% acrylic microfiber, 10% cashmere; 197yd/1¾oz ball.

Rowan Kidsilk Haze
70% kid mohair, 30% silk; 230yd/¾oz ball

Rowan Pure Wool DK
100% wool; 136yd/1¾oz ball.

Jaegar Extra-fine Merino Chunky
100% extra-fine merino wool; 69yd/1¾oz ball

Rowan Scottish Tweed DK
100% wool; 123yd/1¾oz ball.

Debbie Bliss Donegal Tweed Chunky
100 wool; 109yd/3½oz hank

Debbie Bliss Cashmerino Chunky
55% merino wool, 33% microfiber, 12% cashmere blend; 71yd/1¾oz ball.

Debbie Bliss Merino Aran
100% merino wool; 93yd/1¾oz ball.

Anchor Arista
80% viskose 20% polyester; 109yd/¾oz ball.

substituting yarn

If you do decide to use a yarn that is different to the one suggested, please do follow these simple rules before buying it.

Firstly, for a pattern where a specific fit is needed, do use a yarn that is the suggested weight, even if you choose a different brand. If you use a sport-weight where the project asks for a chunky weight, you will run into problems.

Secondly, it is the number of yards of yarn in each ball, not the weight of the ball, that is important. Different brands of yarn, even if they are the same weight, will not necessarily contain the same number of yards of yarn. So you cannot just buy the number of balls the pattern asks for in your substitute yarn: you need to do two sums, but they are simple ones.

Given opposite is the number of yards per ball for the yarns used in the projects. Multiply the appropriate number of yards by the number of balls needed to knit the project. This will give you the total number of yards of yarn you need.

Now check the ball band of your substitute yarn to see how many yards there are in a ball. Divide the total number of yards needed by the number in one ball of the substitute yarn and this will tell you how many balls of that yarn you need to buy.

For example, if the project you have chosen to knit suggests five balls of Debbie Bliss Cashmerino Chunky, but you want to use Rowan Cashsoft Chunky yarn, the sums will be as follows:

- **71 (number of yards of yarn in a ball of Cashmerino Chunky) x 5 (number of balls needed) = 355 (yards of yarn needed to knit the project)**
- **355 (yards of yarn needed to knit the project) ÷ 55 (number of yards of yarn in a ball of Cashsoft Chunky) = 6.5 (number of balls of yarn needed to knit the project)**

You will therefore need to buy seven balls of Rowan Cashsoft Chunky to knit the project.

Before you start knitting the project, you absolutely must knit a gauge swatch in the substitute yarn. Turn to page 116 and read the information on knitting a gauge swatch, then knit one and carefully check that the substitute yarn will achieve the gauge stated in the pattern.

care of knitwear

Having put time and effort into knitting a project, it's worth looking after it properly.

Many modern yarns can be washed in the washing machine on a special wool cycle. However, if your machine doesn't offer that, then you should hand-wash your knitwear.

Firstly, test that the yarn is colorfast by dipping a corner into warm, soapy water and then squeezing the water out onto a clean white cloth. If the color stains the cloth, then wash the item in cold water; if not, then use warm water.

Fill the sink with the appropriate water and add soap flakes or wool detergent. Froth up a lather with your hands. Put the item into the water and gently squeeze it to push the soap into it. Do not leave knitted items to soak for a long time and don't rub the knitting or you risk felting it.

Lift the item out of the water; if it is a garment such as a cardigan, lift it out as a single mass to avoid stretching it. Squeeze the garment to remove excess soapy water, but don't wring it. Fill the sink with clean water (cold or warm as appropriate) and put the item in it. Gently squeeze it to remove the soap suds. Repeat this rinsing process until the water stays clear. Lift the item out and squeeze it again to remove excess water.

Lay the item flat on a thick towel. Roll the towel up and press it firmly to press out as much water as possible. If necessary, repeat with a second towel. Never, ever wring out a piece of knitwear, you can distort the shape very easily.

To dry the knitting, lay it flat and ease it into shape. Lay it on a flat rack or on a flat surface that has been covered with a towel.

Store your knitting flat, not on a hanger, to avoid stretching it. If you pack your knitwear away for the summer, do put some moth protection in with it. You can buy natural protectors that contain few or no chemicals and smell less unpleasant than the chemical versions. Put protection in with silk knitted items as well as woolen ones; moths love silk, too.

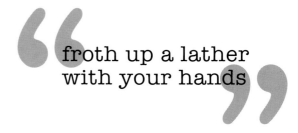

froth up a lather with your hands

abbreviations

Abbreviations are used in knitting patterns to reduce the length of the text. Here is a list of all the abbreviations used in this book.

A, B, C, etc	colors as indicated in the pattern
alt	alternate
approx	approximate
beg	begin, beginning, begins
C6B	cable six (or number stated) back
C6F	cable six (or number stated) forward
cm	centimeter(s)
cont	continue
dec(s)	decrease, decreasing, decreases
DK	double knitting
dpn	double-pointed needle(s)
foll(s)	following, follows
g	gram(s)
in	inch(es)
inc(s)	increase, increasing, increases
incl	including
k2tog	knit two together
k	knit
m	meter(s)
mm	millimeters
M1	make one stitch
oz	ounce(es)
p2tog	purl two together
p	purl
patt(s)	pattern(s)
psso	pass slipped stitch over
rem	remain, remaining
rep(s)	repeat(s)
rev st st	reverse stockinette stitch
RS	right side
skpo	slip one, knit one, pass slipped stitch over
sl	slip
st(s)	stitch(es)
st st	stockinette stitch
tog	together
WS	wrong side
yo	yarn over
*****	repeat instructions between/following * as many times as instructed
[ ]	repeat instructions between[ ] as many times as instructed

needle sizes

Knitting needles come in standard sizes that are recognized all over the world. However, there are three different sizing systems.

US	metric	old UK and Canadian
50	25	-
35	19	-
19	15	-
15	10	000
13	9	00
11	8	0
11	7.5	1
10½	7	2
10½	6.5	3
10	6	4
9	5.5	5
8	5	6
7	4.5	7
6	4	8
5	3.75	9
4	3.5	-
3	3.25	10
2/3	3	11
2	2.75	12
1	2.25	13
0	2	14

weights and lengths

If you need to convert the weights or lengths given in this book, then use the chart below. Whichever system of measurement you use, metric or imperial, do stick with it throughout a project, as changing systems midway can lead to trouble.

oz = g x 0.0352	cm = in x 2.54
g = oz x 28.57	yd = m x 1.0936
in = cm x 0.3937	m = yd x 0.9144

Lowie favorites

Here are some of my favorite pieces from past and present Lowie collections.

Ribbon tie cape –
Winter 2004
Such a statement piece!
The ruffle collar makes
the cape almost
Elizabethan. It's the
perfect cover-up for an
evening out.

" the perfect cover-up for an evening out "

Maxi-scarf – Winter 2006
This chunky scarf featured
at Paris Fashion Week in
the runway show of
the Australian design
sensation, Collette
Dinnigan. Each scarf,
which weighs over 2lb,
has 16-in long fringing
to add to its already
enormous length.

Left: Prom dress –
Winter 2007
This fluorescent pink and
navy blue number is a nod
to both 80s colouring and
50s styling. Combined
with the flight cap and a
diagonally striped scarf
tied up in a side bow, it's
gorgeously comic.

Below: Yellow tunic,
purple snood, and cable
belt – Winter 2006
Cabling is worked through
all three pieces to tie
them together. The cable
on the snood (which
matches the tunic's
sleeves), turns the tunic
into a polo neck.

"a nod to 80s colouring
and 50s styling"

Organic cotton tea dress –
Summer 2007
Lowie is striving as much
as possible to be an
eco-brand and I am very
proud to have used such
lovely quality organic
cotton. With its crochet
sleeves, this dress is a
winner for all lovers of
the vintage look.

resources

USA

Debbie Bliss yarns
Knitting Fever Inc.
P.O. Box 502
Roosevelt
New York 11575
Tel: (516) 546 3600
www.knittingfever.com

Rowan yarns
Westminster Fibers Inc.
4 Townsend West
Suite 8
Nashua, NH 03063
Tel: 603 886 5041
www.westminsterfibers.com

Arista crochet yarn
Coats & Clark
Consumer Services
P.O. Box 12229
Greenville
SC 29612-0229
Tel: (800) 648-1479
www.coatsandclark.com

Canada

Debbie Bliss and Rowan yarns
Diamond Yarns Ltd
155 Martin Ross Avenue
Unit 3
Toronto
Ontario M3J 2L9
Tel: 001 416 736 6111
www.diamondyarn.com

UK

Debbie Bliss yarns
Designer Yarns Ltd
Units 8-10 Newbridge Industrial Estate
Pitt Street
Keighle,
West Yorkshire, BD21 4PQ
Tel: 01535 664222
Fax: 01535 664333
www.designeryarns.uk.com

Rowan yarns
Rowan Yarns and Jaeger Handknits
Green Lane Mill
Holmfirth
West Yorkshire HD9 2DX
Tel: 01484 681881
www.knitrowan.com

Arista crochet yarn
Coats Crafts UK
PO Box 22
Lingfield House
Lingfield Point
McMullen Road
Darlington
County Durham DL1 1YQ
England, United Kingdom
Tel: 01325 394237
www.coatscrafts.co.uk

USEFUL WEBSITES

Adriafil Yarns
www.adriafil.com

Anny Blatt
www.annyblatt.com

Cascade Yarns
www.cascadeyarns.com

Colinette Yarns
www.colinette.com.

Garnstudio
www.garnstudio.com

Karabella Yarns
www.karabellayarns.com

Kollage Yarns
www.kollageyarns.com

Peace Fleece
www.peacefleece.com

Plymouth Yarn Co
www.plymouthyarn.com

Prism Yarns
www.prismyarn.com

Rooster Yarns
www.roosteryarns.com

Tahki
www.tahkistacycharles.com
for stockists.

Texere Yarns
www.texere.co.uk
for stockists.

index

acknowledgments

It's been so much fun making my first book, but I couldn't have done it without the help of the following people: Cindy Richards for believing the book could work; my faithful assistants, Sarah and Ryoko, for being there when needed; Kate Haxell for being an inspiring editor and an amazing source of information at every hour of the day; Penny Hill and Sue Whiting for coming to the rescue with last-minute patterns and knitting; Rachel Myers, Dygo, Asama Uetsuji and Becky Maynes for being such excellent photographers and letting us use their photos on the Lowie favourites pages; Sally Powell for being so organised; Luis Peral-Aranda for making the pages look so fabulous; Ken Harrisson (without whom I would never have got this far); and last (but not least), the ever-cute Elvis the dog.

Additional photography credits: Dygo: pp10–13, pp18–21, pp30–31, pp46–49, pp52–55, p125.
Rachel Myers: p122. Asama Uetsuji: p123, p124 below.